WOMEN UNDER POLYGAMY

WOMEN UNDER POLYGAMY

WALTER M. GALLICHAN

GYAN

Published by

Gyan Publishing House
5, Ansari Road
Daryaganj, New Delhi-110002
Phone: 011-47034999, 9811692060
E-mail: books@gyanbooks.com

Distribution Network
gyanbooks.com
India, USA, Canada, UK, Australia

ISBN: 978-93-7169-874-0 (HB)

First Published, 1914

2nd Impression 2025

Printed at: Gyan Press, Delhi.

WOMEN UNDER POLYGAMY
Author: WALTER M. GALLICHAN

WOMEN UNDER POLYGAMY

TURKISH WOMEN

WOMEN UNDER POLYGAMY

BY

WALTER M. GALLICHAN

With Numerous Illustrations

1915

PREFACE

THE reader of the American Edition of this interesting book will be inclined to ask: "What about the Mormons?" The Latter-day Saints exist in our midst as the only case of the practice of polygamy, after the laboratory method, among a Western people. The account here given of Mormon polygamy is necessarily brief. It may, therefore, be well to supplement it with a fuller account of these "Saints" of whom Mark Twain once observed: "Their creed is singular, and their wives plural."

The Mormons themselves have furnished an answer to what they complained to be the "unaccountable problem" why the Latter-day Saints are "numbered with Indians, Hottentots, Arabs, Turks, Wolverines, and horned cattle." That answer was borrowed from the enemy; it was that "the conduct of Joseph Smith and the other leaders is such that no community of *white* men can tolerate." The conduct the "gentiles" complained of was, of course, the practice of polygamy. This went through three stages: It was first forbidden; next it was practiced before it was preached; lastly it was made not only permissive, but obligatory among the faithful. The documents in the case are significant. The Book of Mormon expressly forbade the practice: "Behold, David and Solomon truly had many wives and concubines, which thing was abominable before me, saith the Lord . . . Wherefore, I, the Lord God, will not suffer that this people shall do like unto them of old. Wherefore, my brethren, hear me, and hearken to the word of the Lord; for there shall not any man among you hath save it be one wife; and concubines he shall have none; for I, the Lord God, delighteth in the chastity of women. And whoredoms are an abomination before me; thus saith the Lord of Hosts."

As if the prohibition of the "Gold Bible" was not enough, the Book of Commandments forbade the same practices. But the third of the canonical books, which in order of time and authority superseded the first two, contains the famous "Revelation on the Eternity of the Marriage Covenant, including Plurality of Wives, given through Joseph, the Seer." The salient passages of this document are there: "As pertaining to the law of the priesthood, if any man espouse a virgin, and desire to espouse another, and the first give her consent; and if he espouse the second, and they are virgins, and have vowed to no other man, then is he justified; he cannot commit adultery, for they are given with him; he cannot commit adultery with that that belongeth unto him and to no one else. And if he have ten virgins given unto him by this law, he cannot commit adultery, for they belong to him, and they are given unto him, therefore is he justified."

It was easy to justify polygamy on paper. It was much harder in reality. But the thing was done. First the Seer's wife had to be appeased. This was accomplished by a special section in the revelation which ran: "Verily, thus saith the Lord unto you, my servant Joseph . . . let mine handmaid, Emma Smith, receive all those that have been given unto my servant Joseph, and which are pure and virtuous before me. . . ." The same procedure was adopted with other women. Thus the confession of Lucy Kimball runs: "President Joseph Smith sought an interview with me, and said: 'I have a message for you. I have been commanded of God to take another wife and you are the woman.' My astonishment knew no bounds. . . . The prophet discerned my sorrow. He saw how unhappy I was . . . and said: 'Although I cannot, under existing circumstances, acknowledge you as my wife, the time is near when we will go beyond the Rocky Mountains and then you will be acknowledged and honored as my wife . . . I will give you until to-morrow to decide this matter. If you reject this message the gate will be closed forever against you.' "

The result of this "command" can be imagined. The woman's surrender was due, as the author suggests, and as I have pointed out in my book, "The Founder of Mormonism," to the hypnotism of a positive personality. The same thing happened with the men. Eliza Snow tells how she requested her "husband," the prophet, to open to her brother, the subject of her plural or "celestial" marriage. "A favorable opportunity soon presented, and, seated together on the bank of the Mississippi River, they had a most interesting conversation. The prophet afterward told me he found that my brother's mind had been previously enlightened on the subject in question. That Comforter which Jesus says shall 'lead into all truth' had penetrated his understanding, and, while in England, had given him an intimation of what at that time was to many a secret. This was the result of living near the Lord."

So much for the personal side in the origin of Mormon polygamy. The doctrinal is equally curious. The Book of Mormon, as we have seen, expressly reprehended the conduct of the Old Testament worthies. But the New Testament was different. As one of the early leaders, Orson Hyde, explained: "It will be borne in mind that, once on a time, there was a marriage in Cana of Galilee; and on a careful reading of that transaction it will be discovered that no less a person than Jesus Christ was married on that occasion. If he was never married, his intimacy with Mary and Martha, and the other Mary also, whom Jesus loved, must have been highly unbecoming and improper, to say the best of it. I will venture to say that, if Jesus Christ was now to pass through the most pious countries in Christendom, with a train of women such as used to follow him, fondling about him, combing his hair, anointing him with precious ointments, washing his feet with tears and wiping them with the hair of their heads, and unmarried, or even married, he would be mobbed, tarred and feathered, and rode, not on an ass, but on a rail. . . . Did he multiply, and did he see his seed? Did he honor his Father's law by complying with it, or did he not? Others may do as they like, but I will not charge our Saviour with neglect or transgression in this or any other duty."

But there was more to the "mystery" of spiritual wifeism than religious sanctions of old. There is a new metaphysics of Mormonism, a philosophical system which presents the very reasons for the faith. The spiritual wife doctrine, according to one of the first believers, was this: "Joseph had a revelation from God that there were a number of spirits to be born into the world before their exaltation in the next; that Christ would not come until all these spirits received or entered their 'tabernacles of clay;' that these spirits were hovering around the world, and at the doors of bad houses, watching a chance of getting into their tabernacles; that God had provided an honorable way for them to come forth—that was, by the Elders in Israel sealing up virtuous women; and as there was no provision made for woman in the Scriptures, their only chance of heaven was to be sealed up to some Elder for time and eternity, and be a star in his crown forever; that those who were the cause of bringing forth these spirits would receive a reward, the ratio of which reward should be the greater or less according to the number they were the means of bringing forth." This raw presentation of pluralism has since been worked up into the finished product of regular church doctrine: "Celestial" marriage, according to the orthodox Saints, opens the way for all women who wish to marry to fill the measure of their creation. . . . It shows how the innumerable creations of God [*i. e.,* this world and other planets] may be peopled with intelligences . . . woman without man and man without woman cannot be saved. The larger the progeny a man has, the greater will be the fulness of his eternal glory.

With the theory of Mormon polygamy before us, it may be interesting to consider its application. The casual visitor in Utah may, at first glance, consider it "one of the finest communities of agriculturists and artisans that the world has seen." But to what is that prosperity due? The Saints claim that their organisation and institutions made the desert to blossom like the rose. But certain economists have pointed out other facts. First it is pointed out that the State of Deseret would have collapsed unless it had been for the influx of Forty Niners, the gold seekers who left much money behind them as they passed through on their way to California. Next, it was only at the beginning that the communistic system of Mormondom at first helped the infant colony, especially in its strife against the federal government. To utilise a phrase of Franklin's: "If they had not hung together, they would have hung separately." But at present the communistic system of the Saints cannot compare in efficiency with the free competitive system of the Gentiles. The Zion Coöperative Mercantile Establishment, for example, does not offer as low prices as the establishment next door. Moreover, the system of tithing, instead of resulting in an accumulation of capital, for the benefit of the contributors, has been wasted in keeping up the harems of the leaders. In short, what was gained in coöperation was lost in cohabitation. This judgment does not apply, of necessity, to the rural districts. As with Mohammedanism so with Mormonism, polygamy is an expensive luxury, to be afforded only by rich dignitaries in the city. But in the country it is different. There it is cheaper to marry a helpmate than to hire "help."

This perhaps explains why, as the author remarks, polygamy has "fallen into disrepute among Mormons themselves." The problem of the hard lot of the farmer's wife is intensified under pluralism. The rural household drudge longs to live in the city. And there, among the Gentiles, she sees that the wife of the monogamist is not only no servant, but an equal partner in the domestic establishment. It is this exclusive matrimonial monopoly, instead of coöperative cohabitation, that makes the Mormon "spiritual" wife envious of her Gentile neighbor.

As for the claim that polygamy drives out prostitution, it depends how one considers the subject, from the individual or the collective point of view. One would hesitate to quote exactly what was said by a daughter of Brigham Young on the witness stand. It was to the effect that if Salt Lake

City were roofed over, it could hardly be called a house of the Lord. On this topic the author might well have added a middle term to his discussion. Polygamy may have driven out prostitution, but it has not driven out promiscuity. There was at one time a literal "stock" exchange among the "cows" and "heifers" as one of the church presidents so delicately referred to the wives and daughters. When divorce could be obtained for so low a fee as ten dollars, it is hard to distinguish between this form of progressive polygamy and plain prostitution.

As to the final claim that the Saints have abandoned the "evils of seduction" the truth of the matter is quite the contrary. In the Mormon public schools coeducation and cohabitation are not so far apart. Add to the sexual curiosity of adolescence the teaching of the "mysteries" of "sealing" and the effect can be left to the imagination.

WOODBRIDGE RILEY.

CONTENTS

CONTENTS

LIST OF ILLUSTRATIONS

WOMEN UNDER POLYGAMY

CHAPTER I

THE ORIGIN OF THE HAREM

AMONG the Western nations there are, no doubt, many unreflective and incurious persons who regard the vast institution of polygamy merely as a part of the faith and practice of the ancient Hebrews, the Hindus, and the Mohammedans of former and modern times. The custom is of far greater antiquity than the older religion of the Jews and the birth of Islam. For the origin of polygamy we must seek among the animal ancestry of mankind.

Many male birds and mammals are instances of that instinct of securing a plurality of sexual companions, which in the view of Voltaire, Schopenhauer, and other philosophers, is the natural impulse of mankind. Leaving for the present, the consideration of Schopenhauer's assumption that every normal man desires more than one wife, let us glance for a moment at the sex-relations of the animals nearest to ourselves in the evolutionary chain.

In the Primates, "the lords of the animal world," we find that the Simiæ, or true apes, possess organs and nervous systems very closely resembling those of the human being. They have also human-like desires and appetites. Yet among the monkeys we note that polygamy is not the invariable form of union; for some of the species are rigidly monogamous. And so with birds, which are, generally speaking, excellent examples of fidelity to a single partner after courtship and pairing.

The stag has his group of hinds; but the blackbird is supposed to pair with one hen for life. The hawks are monogamous. There is sufficient evidence that the polygamous instinct is not general among animals. The farmyard cock and the male grouse are polygamists, but these are exceptions among birds.

Although most of the carnivorous animals are monogamous, the lion sometimes secures more than one mate. The sea-lions are extremely polygamous, and so are some of the seals.

Among birds the polygamic instinct is strongly instanced in the ruffs. The polygamous birds are almost invariably addicted to conflict, and the males are usually bigger and more gaily-feathered than the females. Stags, especially among the red-deer, are very aggressive towards other males, and sometimes their battles end fatally. A young stag will fight for as many hinds as he can obtain;

and the group of females remains his exclusive possession until wrested from him by a more powerful antagonist.

In the marriage customs of mankind we trace, as Goethe said, "the beginning and the end of all culture." The history of civilisation is chiefly the history of the loves of men and women. We must inquire, therefore, into the origin of the widespread polygamy and concubinage, practised from the earliest period of civilisation, as dispassionately as we examine the source of monogamy.

Plurality of wives has been denounced by Schlegel and numerous Western historians and moralists as abominable and unnatural. Are we justified in accepting such condemnation without careful examination of the system? There is not a stable form of sexual morality for all times and all peoples. Sheer biological necessity, quite apart from ethical ideas, has chiefly determined human sexual relationships throughout all the stages of man's development.

Polygamous marriage in ancient communities grew in some instances through a preponderance in the number of women, just as polyandry arose through a preponderance of men in the tribe. This is not the sole and the invariable cause of either kind of marriage, but an excess of one sex over the other is, no doubt, a factor. In the Western nations of to-day, where the female population exceeds the male, there is no sanctioned and recognised polygamy. But there is an irregular form of polyandry exampled in the universal practice of prostitution, and more or less open concubinage.

No doubt, the dominant primitive man resembled the gorilla in his desire to possess more than one wife. The craving for variety in sexual unions is probably as deep-rooted in human nature as the desire to subdue enemies and to reap the wealth of conquest. This impulse of sexual variety is checked and thwarted by various means among masses of the people of the West.

Nevertheless, in spite of religious inhibitions, public opinion, psychic refinement in sexual appetite, poverty, and other obstacles to the gratification of polygamous yearnings, there are many instances of the expression of this innate and imperious passion for variety. Christianity and Christian legislation have not succeeded in annihilating the wandering sexual longings of those men and women in whom basic and pristine emotions survive.

"What is the meaning of maintaining monogamy?" wrote James Hinton. "Do you call English life monogamous?"

Our monogamy is constantly varied by polygyny, or pseudo-polygamy, lacking the sanctions and responsibilities of Mohammedan plurality. Side by side with monogamic marriage, concubinage has always existed. The system was plainly recognised in the ancient laws of Wales. In the Thirteenth Century, in England, the mistress, "the concubina legitima," was often the companion of the wife. There are, indeed, many facts in early Christian history that show an ecclesiastic recognition of the tendency of men towards variety or polygyny.

Even in Puritan times there was a measure of toleration for those who could not remain continent with one woman; for we find a writer, in 1658, asserting that it may be in "every way consistent with the principles of a man fearing God and loving holiness to have more women than one to his proper use."

The aggressive, virile man, who craved plurality of wives, or sexual consorts, was also undoubtedly a lover of the power yielded by possessions. When he stole or purchased women for his harem, he increased his prestige and dignity in the tribe. The passion of acquisitiveness is one of the sources of modern polygamy; and it is frequently this impulse, in England and America, which accounts for the lavish expenditure upon the maintenance of a mistress.

Many men are covetous and greedy by nature. They must own costly things. The complete ownership of a beautiful woman, or of more than one woman, affords them intense pleasure, apart from amatory reasons. This lust for the exclusive ownership of several women dominated the masterful barbarian, and was one of the influences in the institution of the primitive harem system.

The typical polygamous man might be described as highly masculine in all his secondary sexual characteristics. He is predominantly male in a love of authority and of ownership. His instinct is for fighting and subjugation. The early polygamous nations were chiefly martial.[1] The men delighted in warfare, extension of territory, and capture of women, slaves, and spoil.

During this militant period, women conducted those peaceful and pastoral industries which are at the basis of civilisation. They tamed and domesticated animals; they wove the garments, prepared and cooked the food, and tended the infants and the sick. The warrior devoted to Mars returned triumphant from battle to reap his re-

[1] There are modern exceptions, such as the Iroquois Indians, who are monogamic.

ward in the tenderness and caresses of woman.

Wherever maleness predominates in the man, we shall find the polygamous form of marriage among the ancient races as in the primitive communities of to-day. When the necessity for fighting and hunting begins to wane, men occupy themselves, more often, with the industries assigned hitherto to the women of the tribe; and certain of the marked male characteristics undergo a change. At this stage the position of women is usually raised, and by gradual stages she often becomes supreme in power, as in the Matriarchal Period.

With a cessation of the dangers of combat and the chase, more men survive in the community; and there is a tendency towards equalisation in the number of males and females. Celibacy being abhorred as contrary to nature, every man demands his right to a wife, and every woman claims a husband.

In cases where the women are more numerous than the men, among existing primitive people, the practice of polygamy is regarded as a natural necessity. The Esquimaux man of the present day, being a fisher and hunter, is continually at contest with the forces of nature, and therefore subject to mortality from accidents. Many Esquimaux fishermen lose their lives by drowning, and in conflict with animals. The widows are not left to languish in celibacy. A man is always willing to take the husbandless woman into his own home, and to adopt her children; an arrangement which is never resented by his first wife.

Polygamy arose naturally in the barbarous times, when it became imperative to capture women for the propagation of offspring and the maintenance of the group. If the conquering side bore off a large number of women, each man was able to secure three or four wives.

Among the semi-civilised communities of our time, polygyny is far commoner than polygamy. The secondary wife, or concubine, is found amongst the Fijians, the tribes of the Pacific Coast, in Madagascar, in Uganda, Ashanti, and other parts of Africa.

Polygyny is often confused with polygamy; but the distinction is important. A devout Mohammedan, the husband of not more than four wives, duly legitimatized, is, strictly speaking, a polygamist; but the Chinese mandarin—with a legal wife chosen for him by his parents—who takes concubines or inferior wives into his household, may be called a polygynist.

This form of sex union in its most primitive example occurs when several sisters are married to the same man. An instance of such a marriage is to be found in the story of Jacob and Rachel and Leah.

Wake, in his painstaking survey of early marriage customs, states that, in the oldest form of polygyny, all of a man's wives possessed equal rights. In another form there is a favourite, or principal, wife, or wives, and inferior wives, who are sometimes legal wives, and at others serf-wives or concubines.

An economic cause of polygamy must not be overlooked. When the dominant males of a community realised that the men of another group were willing to barter for women instead of fighting for them, they began to trade in their daughters and other women relatives.

In the uncultured nations that bartered their womenfolk, a woman was regarded merely as an article of exchange or sale. Later, however, the purchased woman secures certain important rights. She is not sold body and soul to her purchaser; and a sum of money is settled upon her for sole personal use.

There exists among the Arabs of the White Nile district a rule giving to the purchased girl full liberty on two days of each week. As a wife she is only at the behest of her lord on four days out of the seven. Upon the other day she may even regard herself as free from married fidelity.

Besides their sexual attraction, several wives were valuable to a man in the hunting and battle days. The Sioux Indian is often assisted by his wives in the pursuit of wild animals for food or skins. Women are regarded as business assets. With their help a man can increase his possessions. The Sioux with but one wife remains poor. The housewife cannot leave the cooking and the care of her family for the chase, whereas the fortunate owner of several wives has companions for his hunting.

In Australia, according to Howitt, the natives of the interior obtain as many wives as they can afford, not only from passional ardour, but because they are of use to them. A husband can lend his wives for a gift to young men who are unmarried, and by this means he may acquire property.

The property value of women in primitive societies undoubtedly encouraged plurality of wives. A man was esteemed in proportion to the number of women with whom he cohabited.

Wife purchase is not solely the custom of savage people, nor of living Oriental races. It was a practice of the early English and of all the Teutonic people; and the wedding-ring survives as a symbol of a sale-contract.

Havelock Ellis, quoting from the "Annual Register," for 1767, says that an English bricklayer's labourer sold a woman to a fellow workman "for a quarter guinea and a gallon of beer." We may suppose that the vendor subsequently regretted this transaction; for we read that the woman soon after inherited "£200 and some plate, left her by a deceased uncle in Devonshire."

The masculine desire for more than one wife (polygamy) has been more often expressed than the feminine desire for more than one husband (polyandry). On the whole, it is stated by some authorities on the marriage customs of mankind, that, of the two systems, polygamy is the better for the race. Polygamy served a racial end in early communities, inasmuch as it enabled the most forceful men to beget the largest number of offspring, and so to perpetuate vigorous qualities. Everywhere plurality of wives has been more the mark of a man's success and power in the community than an expression of male sensuality. The great harem represents a man's dignity and position in society, while its maintenance involves a number of strict legal and social obligations towards wives and concubines.

As we shall see, primitive polygamy arose in many tribes through the labour potentiality of women. The chief with the largest number of wives commanded the largest number of assistants in hunting and industry, and sometimes in warfare. The source of polygamy is not invariably amatory; the system has been often forced upon the community through a scarcity of males. In the fighting and hunting age many men died in combat and the chase. But the preponderance of females has not always been brought about by the high mortality among males. There are races that tend to reproduce more females than males, or more males than females. Whenever the balance of the sexes is disturbed, plurality of males naturally results.

The chief cause of polygamy in the past was economic. Moral reprobation of the practice has often been based on the assumption that polygamous marriage grew solely from the "vices" or the sexual acquisitiveness of men. This is not proved in the case of primitive polygamy. And though there is ample testimony showing that savage races are far less incontinent than highly civilised people, it is rarely that celibacy exists among them. Polygamy provides mates for the superfluous women of the group. Polyandry supplies partners for the redundant men. Celibacy is a state regarded by primitive people as unnatural, or as contrary to moral law, and according to such a conception, avoidance of celibacy must be provided for by an adjustment of the marriage customs.

C. N. Starcke finds in the desire of primitive fathers to own many children one of the chief incentives to polygamous marriage.[2] Naturally, the man with the largest number of wives will possess the most numerous progeny. The savage with a goodly number of children owns a retinue of companions for the chase and of workers in the fields and the home.

The craving for dignity, power and riches is clearly one of the main sources of polygamy and concubinage. It has been reiterated again and again by ill-informed writers that "men's lust" alone is the cause of plural marriage. Investigation proves, however, that it is a minor factor, at any rate in polygamy of early ages and among existing primitive tribes.

It is important to note that monogamy has always accompanied polygamy. Obviously, even when women have been redundant, there has not existed a sufficient number to enable each man to possess several wives. Polygamy is the luxury of

[2] "The Primitive Family."

the prosperous, and it stands for property-ownership. The poor man is bound to practise monogamy. Among some African tribes, the greed of the king and the chiefs, in the acquisition of large harems, actually condemns a part of the male population to celibacy.

" Polygamy," says Starcke, "can never have been the normal condition of a tribe, since it would have involved the existence of twice as many women as men."

It is often assumed that women in polygamic countries are the mere slaves of men, and that they are forced into plural marriage. This is scarcely the truth. Women as well as men have determined the forms of the sexual relationships in communities. Among animals living in polygamy, compulsion on the part of the males is very seldom apparent in their conduct towards the females. The sea lions are a marked exception. But the stag and other polygamous animals woo and incite rather than impel the hinds to join his troop. It has been noticed generally by naturalists and hunters that the females voluntarily attach themselves to the powerful younger males owning several mates.

As there is not a wide difference between the instincts of the animal and that of primitive men, it seems beyond question that the great bulk of the women of the tribe do not disapprove of polygamous marriage. Doubtless there are a few malcontents, but the mass of the women approve the system. There is plenty of evidence in this matter. Dr. Livingstone is by no means the only traveller who has heard primitive women declare that they would not live in a country where a man is only permitted to marry one woman.

CHAPTER II

THE ANCIENT HAREM

I. BABYLON

AMONG the ruins of the noble palaces of Assyria were carvings depicting the leading of men and women captives into the cities. At Khorsabad one of these interesting relics showed plainly the figures of women and eunuchs. "For lo! our fathers have fallen by the sword, and our sons and our daughters and our wives are in captivity."

That the harem existed in Nineveh is proved by the testimony of its mural sculpture and the inscriptions deciphered by Colonel Rawlinson and other investigators. This earliest recorded empire came to an end with the great Sardanapalus, probably in 820 B.C., who, upon the sacking of the city by Arbaces, concealed himself in his palace, and set fire to it. With his concubines, eunuchs and slaves he perished; and the Assyrian Empire of Babylon and Nineveh were formed after his death.

Herodotus tells us that the seat of the government, after the downfall of Nineveh, was transferred to Babylon. The city stood in a wide plain, covering a great area, and in its extent and the beauty of its architecture, Babylon surpassed all other cities. A moat and a high wall encompassed the city. In the wall, at the end of each street, were gates of brass. The royal residence and harem stood in the midst of a fortified enclosure.

The temple of Jupiter Belus was an immense square building. In one of the towers was a temple, wherein no mortal might pass the night except a native woman chosen by the deity from the whole nation. This priestess, who was a vestal, was said to be visited by the god himself.

In Babylon women were queens and priestesses, and held other exalted positions. The goddess was more honoured than the god. Women owned property and had equal rights with men. The Queen Semiramis had immense sway; and greater still was the power of Nitocris, who, according to Herodotus, enlarged and fortified the city and showed a wonderful capacity for engineering and the planning of canals and reservoirs.

By the famous Code of Hammurabi, marriage by purchase and polygamy were permitted in Babylon. But wives could not be divorced at the caprice of the husband, and the marriage dowry given to the bride by her father could not be taken from her even though she were divorced. Concubinage was allowed by the Code, the secondary wife, or concubine, ranking as subordinate to the chief wife.

If a man desired a maiden for his wife, he approached her parents first, and the prospective bride had no voice in the contract. Herodotus describes a custom of the Babylonian villagers that recalls the old-time hiring fairs of England. Once a year all the girls of a marriageable age were collected together in an open space, surrounded by a crowd of men. One by one the damsels were put up for sale, the more comely being first offered to the bidders. The wealthiest men naturally secured the most beautiful wives. After the disposal of the handsome women, their plain sisters were sold by auction; but in this case they were given to poor men, and the successful bidder was one who would accept the lowest dowry. This sum was paid out of the sale of the beautiful maidens.

Until the buyer of a girl had given full assurance that he would marry her legally, he was not permitted to carry her away. In the event of disharmony in the married life, the wife could be freed from the tie by the return of the purchase money. "Such," writes the historian, "was their best institution. It has not, however, continued to exist." At a later period, after defeats in warfare and impoverishment, the poorer classes resorted to the selling of their daughters in prostitution.

Herodotus refers to the sacred prostitution of women at the Temple of Mylitta, the Venus of the Babylonians. Generally speaking, prostitution is comparatively uncommon in polygamous countries, and its introduction often arises from the coming of strangers from the monogamous nations. The religious rite observed in the Babylonian temple was by no means a purely commercial transaction. Once in her life every woman in ancient Babylon was compelled to sit in the Temple of Mylitta until chosen by a man. The wealthy women came in carriages attended by their servants. The women sat in a row, and the men passed up and down. When a man had made his choice, he threw a piece of silver into the woman's lap, and she was bound to accompany him. After "absolving herself from her obligation to the goddess," the woman returned home, and was regarded as chaste. The plain-featured and the deformed were often obliged to remain in the temple for a considerable time. "Some wait for a space of three or four years," relates Herodotus. The money given to the women was devoted to the temple of the goddess.

Herodotus describes this custom of the Babylonians as "most disgraceful." But he does not seem to have inquired into its origin and full significance. It was the fervent belief of many ancient societies that procreation is sacred, and a tribute to the gods. They believed also that the rite in the temple favoured the fertility of women.

Professor Frazer, in "Adonis, Attis, Osiris," says: "We may conclude that a great mother goddess, the personification of all the reproductive energies of nature, was worshipped under different names, but with a substantial similarity of myth and ritual by many peoples of Western Asia; that associated with her was a lover, or rather series of lovers, divine yet mortal, with whom she mated year by year, their commerce being deemed essential to the propagation of animals and plants, each in their several kind; and further that the fabulous union of the divine pair was simulated, and, as it were, multiplied on earth by the real, though temporary union of the human sexes at the sanctuary of the goddess for the sake of thereby ensuring the fruitfulness of the ground and the increase of man and beast."

The rite of Mylitta was designed as a benefit to the woman-devotee. When the man placed the coin in the woman's lap, he said: "May the goddess be auspicious to thee," referring, no doubt, to her increased potentiality as a mother after the sacred ceremony. Similar rites were practised by the Egyptians, the Romans, in the worship of Priapus, the Corinthians, and among the priestesses of Cyprus.

In Lydia it was the custom of girls to prostitute themselves for the purpose of securing a marriage-portion. Frazer is of the opinion that this was a development of sacred prostitution. At first the money is offered to the god, but later it is used by the woman as a marriage-portion. The practice survives to this day in Japan.[1]

The secularisation of prostitution followed gradually upon the decay of religious and symbolic prostitution among the Eastern nations. Once a ceremony of holy and solemn import, it degenerated into a mere traffic for money, and is now a commercial institution of every monogamous country.

In the harems of Babylon, the wives held considerable power and high status. Nor were the concubines the mere chattels of their masters. The Hammurabi Code had important clauses respecting the treatment of inferior wives. If a man determined to dismiss a concubine, he was compelled to pay her "the usufruct of field, garden, and goods," to maintain and educate her children.

[1] See chapter on "Japan."

A bride put away on the ground of sterility, or for another cause, was entitled to the price originally paid for her. If there was no bride-price, the husband paid her one mina of silver; and in the case of a poor man one-third of a mina of silver.

In regard to faithless wives in the harem, the law was not liberal. The woman who had "belittled her husband," or "played the fool," was sent away without compensation or held as the slave of a new wife. An errant wife was condemned to death by drowning, a favourite Oriental punishment for women.

II. ANCIENT EGYPT

"Among the Egyptians," wrote Diodorus, "the woman rules over the man." The existence of the harem in a nation so distinguished as ancient Egypt for a recognition of sex-equality, is somewhat bewildering at the first thought.

Let us remember that polygamy from the earliest times has been the privilege and the luxury of the rich. It was never the practice of a vast mass of the population in polygamous countries. Therefore, in speaking of such countries, we must not lose sight of the fact that the bulk of women are outside of the harems. It is also necessary that we should recognise the constant recruiting of the inmates of the harem by the importation of alien women.

Hammurabi, the great law-maker of the Babylonians, who held power for forty-three years, published a number of regulations relating to marriage. Adultery was punishable by the death of both persons by drowning. Provision was made for the desertion of wives. "If a man has abandoned his city, and absconded, and after that his wife has entered the house of another, if that man comes back and claims his wife, because he had fled and deserted his city, the wife of the deserter shall not return to her husband." A wife or a concubine who had borne children could not be sent away from the harem without the return of her dowry, and she was at liberty to marry again. Incest incurred a penalty of death, either by drowning or burning, according to the severity of the crime.

The law of Hammurabi was very rigid in regard to the descent of property through the mother.

"If a man has married a wife and she has borne children, and that woman has gone to her fate, then her father has no claim upon her dowry. The dowry is her children's."

Mr. Chilperic Edwards, author of "The Oldest Laws in the World," writes, in his notes on the Hammurabi Code, that many of the stories of

Herodotus about the women of Babylon are fables. "The Babylonian woman was given in marriage by her father or brothers. The suitor, or his family, paid a certain sum as 'bride-price,' the amount being often handed over in instalments. The bride's father gave her a 'dowry,' which usually, but not necessarily, included the 'bride-price.' The bridegroom might also make his bride a 'settlement.'"

"The status of the concubine is not clear. She does not seem to be necessarily of lower rank, like the Roman, but was a secondary spouse. Like the chief wife she carried bride-price and dowry, and we may assume that she possessed the same rights as the chief wife in regard to maintenance and participation in the husband's estate."

A humane measure for the annulment of marriage on the ground of incompatibility is recorded in the following clause:

"If a woman hate her husband, and say 'Thou shalt not possess me,' the reason for her dislike shall be inquired into. If she be careful, and has no fault, but her husband takes himself away and neglects her, then that woman is not to blame. She shall take her dowry and go back to her father's house." [2]

In the Egypt of ancient days the mass of the peo-

[2] "The Oldest Laws in the World."

ple laboured for the mere maintenance of existence, and bowed beneath the stern common lot of the multitude in most civilised nations. Family life among the humble was on a very different plane from the luxurious lives of the influential and the wealthy. But in happy domesticity the Egyptians excelled all peoples. The women were the beloved of their husbands, the mistresses of the house. Innumerable are the precepts to husbands, urging them to bestow tenderness and affection upon their wives, to cherish them in every manner, and to honour all women.

The marriage contracts, in the days of the highest culture in Egypt, prove conclusively that women were more favoured than men. Purchase-marriage became a form only, for the bride-price was given to her, and the wife's property was entirely her own to enjoy and dispense as she chose. In the event of separation, the wife retained her possessions. A woman who left her husband was entitled to all that was her own, and in some instances the wife was endowed with the whole of her husband's belongings.[3]

Children were carefully and lovingly tended by both parents. Even the child of a slave woman

[3] See "The Truth About Woman," C. Gasquoine Hartley (Mrs. Walter M. Gallichan).

was legitimate and accorded equitable rights. The woman who had wandered from the strict path of chastity was not scorned nor made an outcast. Petah Hotep declared that such misfortune should be softened by the kindness of the man who had consorted with her. He was enjoined to shelter her and "be kind to her for a season," and to "send her not away."

The wives living in polygamy had each their own house; their children were endowed, and their property-rights were well-defined. Instead of being at the beck and call of her husband at any time, the woman received him in her own home as an invited guest.

Three centuries ago, in France, certain sage doctors conferred together in order to decide whether women were of the same species as men. In Egypt, long before the advent of Christianity, society had raised women to dignity and almost to adoration. Before we speak of the inevitable degradation of women under a system of polygamy, it will be well to reflect upon the feminism of the ancient Egyptians.

The splendour of the old palaces of Egypt have been often described. Kings occupied magnificent residences, to which temples were attached. The palace had spacious courts and pavilions, and numerous apartments, beautifully adorned with sculpture in relief and with paintings. In the scented and sequestered gardens, there were bowers and sparkling fountains; and rare trees and imported plants flourished.

Surrounded by his wives, children, concubines and slaves, the monarch lived a complete autocrat and the head of a large family.

Women were in constant attendance on the king. When he went out in the city, slaves bore him in a decorated palanquin, or he rode in a resplendent coach. Musicians, singers, and men and women dancers entertained the sovereign in his leisure hours. We read that the royal parents were much attached to their children, and that the king joined in the games of the nursery.

It is clear that when the Egyptians became pacific, women enjoyed the social, civic and domestic advantages which were denied to them during the militant period. The Greek travellers in Egypt were surprised at the independence of the women. It is doubtful whether, at the highest stage in their culture, the Greeks approached the Egyptian ideal of family life.

With the example of ancient Egypt before us, can we assert justly that the position of women has been always debased under polygamous marriage?

Moslem polygamy has its evils. But who can maintain that a sense of justice to women and a true regard for her social and personal well-being has always been a conspicuous virtue of the monogamic communities?

A DAUGHTER OF EGYPT

CHAPTER III

MOHAMMED AND POLYGAMY

WITH the coming of the great Prophet of Islam polygamy in the East received a new seal. The worship of several deities was impeached by the reformer as false and injurious, and a monotheistic creed was substituted by the teaching of the Koran.

A founder of a new faith, however sincere and ardent his belief in revelation, is unable to detach from his inspiration the influence of national custom and tradition. Polygamy was a fixed and popular institution, venerated for its antiquity.

Probably no other system of sexual relationship ever presented itself to the mind of the prophet, except as an instance of the rankest heresy or sin. As an iconoclast vowed to the destruction of the old faiths, Mohammed had studied diligently the sacred writings of the Hebrews. In their Scriptures he read that the patriarchs and monarchs followed the rule of the Eastern nations in plural marriage. His compatriots also practised polygamy. When had the custom been forbidden? Therefore, under the approval of Allah, plurality of wives was plainly permissible. The faithful were instructed that they might take "two, or three, or four, and not more women as wives." Provision was made also for the ancient practice of concubinage. The possession of all women captured in battle, or obtained by purchase, was allowed.

Divorce being sanctioned by the law of the Koran, a devout Moslem is empowered to marry a succession of women; although the number at one time is restricted to four. In the sacred writings, it is laid down that a man may dismiss and repudiate his wives without always showing a definite cause. On the other hand, legal separation, even for adultery, is not so easy as it appears.

Mohammed, whose first occupation was that of a camel driver to a wealthy widow, Khadija, was himself the husband of eleven wives, though not all at the same time, during the years of his mission. His mistress, Khadija, was his first spouse, and he had no other during her life. Special revelations were granted to the prophet as divine sanction for his excess in the number of his wives. But we must not suppose that Mohammed was exceptionally voluptuous. He had led a temperate and almost ascetic youth. His diet was spare, and he often shared his meals with poorer brethren.

Antagonists in the matter of belief have united in according fervent sincerity to Mohammed.

Wellhausen says rightly that the prophet's sheer honesty of aim is proved by his voluntary subjection to the prejudice and the persecution of the people of Mecca, his native city. His virtues were courage, determination, humility in the hour of greatness, courtesy, and generosity.

Judged from the standpoint of Christian monogamic principles, the marriage rules of Mohammed "render the Christian ideal of domestic life an impossibility." Such is the view of Mr. J. W. H. Stobart, the author of "Islam and its Founder." We have seen, however, that "the ideal of domestic life" as upheld in Egypt, was humane, and perhaps the best that the world has known.

But let us examine the position of women in polygamy as permitted by the founder of the Moslem religion. It is commonly declared that women are excluded from the Paradise of the Mohammedans. This is untrue. We are told distinctly that "God will lead the believers of both sexes to the gardens of delight."

The law of the Koran referring to adultery is perhaps less primitive in its severity than that of Moses. Women are, of course, the most frequent delinquents in this offence, because polygamy practically liberates men from temptation. Adultery is punishable by death or life-long imprisonment. But very conclusive proof is required before condemnation. There must be four eye-witnesses to the act. Needless to say, the conviction of offenders is rarely secured.

Regarding illicit intercourse between the sexes, the Mohammedan code is extremely austere. Sir William Muir states justly that "the gross and systematic immorality in certain parts of every Euro pean community may be regarded by the Christian with shame and confusion," and contrasted with "a certain negative virtue" of continence among the followers of Islam.[1]

Although theoretically a Mohammedan may repudiate his wife on a trivial plea, the Koran teaches forbearance to the married. "If a woman fear ill-usage or aversion from her husband, it shall be no crime in them if they agree the matter amicably between themselves; for a reconciliation is better than a separation."

That the wives of the harem possess many rights

[1] The Koran contains very explicit teaching on the preservation of chastity. An aspersion of unchastity upon innocent women was punishable by scourging. Promiscuous sexual relationships are denounced; but a man may cohabit with his slave women or concubines. Strict chastity is enjoined upon Moslem women. Such absolute continence is, however, not considered within the reach of men.

and privileges is beyond question. Very frequently they are the close companions of their husbands, the advisers, and the arbiters in domestic affairs.

The Moorish wives of the khalifs of Spain were frequently women of character and culture; and we read of their devotion to their husbands. Moon, the spouse of Ibn-Hajjaj, of Seville, wrote to her husband: "In all the West I find no right noble man save Ibrahim, but he is nobility itself. When one has known the delight of living with him, to dwell in any other land would be misery."

Kalam, a beauty of the Court of Abd-er-Rahman II., of Cordova, was one of several favoured and cultured women of the harem. She was a poet and a wonderful musician. Tarib, a much-loved concubine, was also greatly honoured by the monarch, who proclaimed her virtues and her loveliness in verse.

Strict modesty was inculcated amongst early Moslems. In pre-Mohammedan days, the preservation of modesty was marked among the Arabs. The Sunna code enjoins that a man should not uncover himself, even when alone, for nakedness was abhorrent to God. We may recall Job's atonement for this offence. Women, when in grief for the loss of a relative by death, expressed their emotion by uncovering the bosom, and often by tearing their garments. A man forbidden to wreak vengeance on an aggressor, showed his annoyance by exposing those parts of the body usually concealed. Such exposures are manifestations of ritual, and have nothing to do with lasciviousness. On certain occasions, the Hebrew prophets cast off their clothing, as a symbol or demonstration of emotion.

Special regulations guarded the pregnant woman and the mother during the period of suckling. Lactation is often prolonged for three years in the East, and, during the exercise of this function, women are compelled to live as celibates. As this would involve sexual abstinence on the part of the husband of one wife, we have here, in part, the origin of the sanction of polygamy. But this injunction does not account for polygamous marriage. Its sources, as I have indicated, sprang from our animal ancestry and primitive appetite.

Although cleanliness of the body was taught, the public bath was not recommended. Mohammed, who probably held the common belief that baths are haunted by evil spirits, forbade this ablution in public. Later, however, he relaxed this rule, and men and women were allowed to bathe, provided they wore loin cloths.

"Whatever woman enters a bath the devil is with her," declared the prophet. Nevertheless, the *hamman,* or bath, became a popular institution of Mohammedanism. The habit of mixed bathing may have been adapted from the Romans. In ancient Pompeii there were three sumptuous public baths.

Christianity abolished the bath. The first saints realised clearly that the cleanness of the skin, produced by bathing, friction, and unguents, was a stimulant to passion. St. Paula reproved her nuns for scrupulous washing, averring that "the purity of the body and its garments means the impurity of the soul." In mediæval Europe, as Lecky points out, the dirtiest of religious devotees were the most honoured for their saintliness. The monks in the Middle Ages bathed only twice a year. It was better to be filthy externally than concupiscent within.

The Christian religion was a reaction and protest against the excesses of Greece and Rome. Frequent ablution, with its tonic effect on the whole system, was practised in the classic times for another reason besides cleanliness. In denouncing the bath, the early Christian teachers aimed at the lessening of sensuality. Under Henry II. of England, baths were recognised legally as brothels. There were several public baths in Southwark at this date.

Among the Moslems the purification of the body was a rite, and we find, throughout the whole dominion of the Mohammedan faith, an intense devotion to the bath. In the wonderful Moorish cities of Spain there were baths in every quarter. The "Turkish bath," with its massage, friction, sweating, and stimulation of the skin, was no doubt designed for other purposes besides ablution.

Celibacy is regarded with pious horror by true believers in Allah. E. W. Lane, author of "Manners and Customs of the Modern Egyptians," found hostility among his neighbours in Egypt because he was unmarried. Difficulties were placed in the way of obtaining a house, and Lane was told that the purchase of a female slave would remove all disabilities. A sheikh besought him to marry a handsome young widow, who was quite willing to be divorced at the end of the visitor's two years' sojourn, or whenever it might suit him.

The avoidance of the sin of celibacy is not difficult in the East. In Egypt, the woman who said, "I give myself up to thee," to a man who desired her as wife, was allowed to marry, even without witnesses, if none could be found. Illicit unions are, therefore, uncommon even to-day.

Oriental male supremacy is expressed clearly in the description of Paradise. In the material heaven prepared for men of this faith, the poorest man is rewarded with seventy-two beautiful brides. The virgins of Paradise are termed *houris,* or *hooreeyehs.* Besides possessing these heavenly spouses, a man may renew his marriage with the wives who have preceded him into elysium. To the Mohammedan woman, Paradise offers no such allurements. She will dwell there as she dwelt on earth, one of many wives.

The man translated to eternal bliss will live in a tent spangled with the costliest jewels, and will eat his delicate meals on plates of gold; while his ears are enraptured by the music of Israfeel, "whose heartstrings are a lute." He will not experience satiety in sensual pleasures. If he pleases, he may beget children. Wine of the most luscious vintage will be his daily beverage, and he may drink of it freely.

Modern exponents of the teaching of Mohammed state that the prophet taught equality between men and women in married life. The salient rights of women under Moslem law are as follows:—[2]

Chastity is enjoined upon men as well as women.

Every wife has her own dower, servants and apartments.

The marriage settlement must be returned in full upon divorce or separation.

At the death of the husband, wife recovers all of her dower and part of her husband's estate.

A wife may incur necessary debts in her husband's name.

A virgin of adult age cannot be compelled to marry.

A divorced woman, or a widow, may marry again.

A woman pays only half of a fine paid by a man for legal offences.

Women must not be killed in warfare.

A wife may, with her husband's consent, seek for divorce.

No wife can be convicted of adultery without the actual evidence of four witnesses.[3]

The legal and social disabilities of the women of Islam are:—

[2] See Syed Ameer Ali's contribution to "The Dictionary of Islam."

[3] "Personal Laws of the Mohammedans"—Ameer Ali.

No woman can object to be one of four wives, nor to the number of concubines maintained by her husband.

Wives may be chastised. We are informed that such punishment is rare.

Women cannot give evidence as witnesses in law courts.

A wife must obey her husband implicitly.

Wives can be repudiated for several causes. Such repudiation is, however, not very common, and Mohammed warned husbands against discharging their wives through caprice or for insufficient reasons. The secluded life of the harem, and the lack of social intercourse with men, except husbands and relatives, tends to narrow the intelligence of women, and their outlook upon life is circumscribed.

In some respects, Mohammed improved the status of women. Before his mission there was considerable licence and a kind of sexual anarchy. It would appear, from certain old Arabian proverbs, that before Islam, women were regarded as malign beings and greatly inferior to men. For example, it was said that:—

"Women are the whips of Satan."

"Obedience to a woman will have to be repented of."

"What has a woman to do with the councils of a nation?"

"Trust neither a king, a horse, nor a woman."

"Our mother forbids us to err, and runs into error."[4]

We find a somewhat higher conception of woman in a Mohammedan saying: "A good wife is as a mother for affection and tenderness; as a slave-girl for content and attentions; as a friend for concord and sincerity." It must be noted that this appraisement embodies docility and obedience, and is entirely in the spirit of the patriarchal rule in families. There is, however, some recognition of companionship between husband and wife.

In "The Crescent and the Cross," Warburton says that Moslem women do not show any discontent with their condition. They like to be watched and guarded closely, and discern no "degradation" in the life of seclusion in the harems. No doubt this is true in regard to the majority of women in the East. The majority everywhere are, as a rule, fairly satisfied with their position. But it is beyond question that dissatisfaction exists among many educated women in Mohammedan countries. There is a "feminist movement" in every civilised state; and educated women in Turkey and Egypt

[4] Dictionary of Islam.

and India hold meetings to-day to discuss the rights of their sex. Some of these conclaves are attended by men, who listen attentively to the pleas and arguments of the women.

While we must grant that there was a stage in pre-Moslem times, in Egypt, Arabia, and Palestine, in which women seem to have occupied an inferior station, the attitude of men was not usually contemptuous or harsh. Woman has always been endowed with mysterious, and often sacred, attributes. Amongst the ancient Arabs the touch of a woman could save a malefactor on the way to execution. So strong was this belief that criminals were led through streets blindfolded.

CHAPTER IV

ANCIENT JEWISH POLYGAMY

AMONG the Semitic people more than one kind of marriage existed. Jacob was the husband of two sisters, and Amram, the father of Moses, married his aunt. The greatest of the Jewish saints were polygamists, and many owned concubines and slave-women. David possessed both wives and concubines. Solomon was the lord of seven hundred wives and three hundred concubines.

Purchase-marriage was the custom; the Hebrew parent was allowed to sell his daughter as a wife, concubine, or maid-servant. The purchaser could dismiss the wife or handmaiden at will. Plurality of wives was also maintained, as in Babylon and Egypt, by the capture of women in warfare.

When Moses conquered the Midianites, he commanded: "Now, therefore, kill every male among the little ones, and kill every woman that hath known man by lying with him. But all the women children that hath not known man by lying with him keep alive for yourselves."

The price paid for a wife in the time of Hosea was fifteen pieces of silver and a homer-and-a-half of barley. If the buyer grew tired of the woman, he had merely to publish the fact that she had "no favour in his eyes," and send her from the home. When a husband conceived suspicion of his wife's infidelity, he was permitted to subject her to a barbarous form of trial by ordeal.

The Jews remained a semi-barbaric race when Babylon and Egypt were hoary nations. The position of their women was greatly inferior in every respect to that of the women of ancient Babylon. Up to the Fifth Century, B.C., polygyny of an almost primitive character survived among the Hebrew people. The practice was not even reprobated by some of the early Christian reformers. It lingered till the Reformation, and was permitted by Martin Luther.

The priestess had wielded power in the old civilisations of the East; but, under the rule of St. Paul, Christian women were even forbidden to speak in the churches. The celibate life was exalted. Later, St. Gregory of Nyssa taught that wedlock is the outcome of iniquity. St. Augustine, who believed in woman's inferiority, declared that bigamy might be permitted if a wife was sterile.

The Jewish harem reached its highest importance and splendour in the time of David and Solomon. David first married Michal, the daughter of Saul, who, after a quarrel, transferred Michal to another husband. Abigal was the next bride of David, and afterwards he formed an adulterous union with the lovely Bathsheba, the wife of Uriah. In his palace were many concubines. Ten of these women misconducted themselves with the king's son Absalom, and as a punishment they were imprisoned for the rest of their lives.

Chastity was inculcated by Moses and Solomon, and fornication was condemned. "Do not prostitute thy daughter to cause her to be a whore, lest the land fall into whoredom, and the land become full of wickedness." (Leviticus 19-29.) Solomon, in the seventh chapter of Proverbs, warns young men against "the strange woman." "Let not thine heart decline to her ways, go not astray in her paths."

In the courts of Baal and Asherah there are distinct traces of ancient Phallicism, and this worship survived till the time of Joshua. The temple of Solomon was of Phœnician character, and the decorations were Phallic. Jeremiah complains that the people "defiled the land, and committed adultery with stones and with stocks." The worship of Priapus is mentioned by Ezekiel (xvi.-17), and such worship of sexual images is referred to in Deuteronomy iv., 16.

Sacred prostitution was known among the Jews, as both Kuenen and Kalisch testify. The latter writer says: "The unchaste worship of Ashtarte, known also as Beltis and Tannais, Ishtar, Mylitta, and Anaitis, Asherah, and Ashtaroth, flourished among the Hebrews at all times, both in the kingdom of Judah and Israel; it consisted in presenting to the goddess who was revered as the female principle of conception and birth, the virginity of maidens as a first-fruit offering; and it was associated with the utmost licentiousness. This degrading service took such deep root that in the Assyrian period it was soon extended by the adoption of new rites borrowed from Eastern Asia, and described by the name of "Tents of the Maidens." [1]

The Song of Solomon, one of the oldest books of the Bible, has been ascribed to the same writer as the Book of Ecclesiastes. Some critics have urged that "the Song of Songs" was a bridal poem celebrating the marriage of Solomon with the daughter of Pharaoh. Whoever the author may have been, the Song of Solomon conveys instructive evidence of the strongly erotic conception of women among the Jews. The poem abounds in sensuous images and rapturous delight in the physical charm of women. This fine relic of ancient Oriental litera-

[1] "Bible Studies."—J. M. Wheeler.

ture was forbidden by the Jewish Church to readers under thirty years of age, on account of its amatory character. The outspokenness of certain passages merely reveals the ordinary Eastern conception of women and love.

The fair damsel of Shulam, who speaks in the Song of Solomon, is an instance of a Hebrew woman's recoil against enforced polygamy. She had been captured and taken to the king's harem, and a place of honour was offered to her. But the Shulamite maid loved a shepherd youth of her native country. The monarch tries all the arts of wooing, and promises precious gifts; but the girl bears in her heart a deep love for her shepherd swain. Even when the king offers to make her the chiefest of "three score queens and four score concubines and virgins without number," the daughter of Shulam still pines for her own land and the caresses of her chosen lover.

In this story we have one of the few Old Testament instances of a preference for the single love-union, and an illustration of the constancy of a woman to her humble suitor, whom she values more than all the privileges and delights of the royal harem.

Four wives were permitted to each man by the old Hebrew teachers. A king might marry eighteen women. Divorce was easily obtained by men, one of the grounds being ugliness in a wife.

Among the Jews professing the faith of Islam, polygamy is still practised in Jerusalem.[2] The conditions of harem life are like those prevailing in Turkey and Egypt. There is a tendency to adopt Western fashions in dress, and the women are clad in Parisian gowns. Marriage is followed by seven days of feasting. The bridegroom hangs swords from the bride's neck, as a sign that she is under his authority. As elsewhere in the East, the wife is heavily perfumed on the bridal day, and her nails and toes are stained with henna.

A. Goodrich Freer says that the children of the Jewish Mohammedans are treated affectionately by their parents, and that there is improvement in the education of girls.

[2] "Inner Jerusalem"—A. Goodrich Freer.

CHAPTER V

THE WOMEN OF INDIA

AMONG the people of our Indian Empire exist all forms of the sex-relationship from polyandry to polygamy. For the student of marriage customs this is a great field for inquiry. India fascinates and bewilders.

In this vast peninsula, we rule over a population of over two-hundred-and-ninety-four millions; a people speaking more than one-hundred-and-forty languages, and adhering to differing traditions and practices. Seventy per cent. of the natives are followers of the Hindu religion. There are over sixty-two millions of Mohammedans; over nine millions Buddhists, mostly in Burma; and more than two millions professing the Christian creed. Besides these believers, there are thousands of Sikhs, Parsees, Jains, and small sects holding various tenets.

The popular faith of India is Hinduism, a creed of pantheism mingled with the worship of many deities. Dominating all other gods is the universal Brahman. The religion is almost incomprehensible to the Western mind. Its keynote is a philosophic pessimism. Life must be endured;

GIRLS OF NORTHERN INDIA

existence is not a boon in itself. "In the union of soul and body lies the source of human misery."

In India there are some millions of widows of the Hindu faith, forbidden by religion to marry a second husband. There are one thousand men to about nine hundred women. Marriage is enjoined upon all adults except widows and religious celibates.

The ethics of Hinduism may perhaps be summed up in this passage from the sacred writings:—

"Joy, pleasure, nobility, enlightenment and happiness also, absence of stinginess, absence of fear, contentment, faith, forgiveness, courage, harmlessness, equability, truth, straightforwardness, absence of wrath, absence of calumniation, purity, dexterity, valour."

Parents and women are to be held in honour:—

"By honouring his father, his mother, and his teacher, all that ought to be done by man is accomplished; that is clearly the highest duty; every other act is a subordinate duty."

"Where women are honoured there the gods are pleased, but where they are not honoured, no sacred rite yields rewards."

"He only is a perfect man who consists of three persons united—his wife, himself, and his offspring."

"He who has unjustly forsaken his wife shall put on an ass's skin with the hair turned outside, and lay in seven houses, saying: 'Give alms to him who forsook his wife.' That shall be his livelihood for six months."

Miss Flora Annie Steel, who possesses an intimate knowledge of Indian life, has said that the average British view of the position of women under Hinduism is "simply appalling" for its ignorance. This author declares that she never knows whether "to laugh or cry at—let us say—a Zenana meeting in some sleepy, self-satisfied, little English village, where a select company of British matrons and spinsters sit in judgment on polygamy with an inward reminiscence of Bluebeard, or shudder at suttee as if they could see no beauty in self-sacrifice."

In 1906, Margaret E. Noble, the Sister Nivedita, published a highly interesting book of intimate Hindu impressions entitled "The Web of Indian Life." The picture that she draws of the status of the Indian woman is fascinating, and, to Western minds, very astonishing. There is no doubt that the writer's lively prejudice has inspired her enthusiastic praise for everything Indian. She applauds the system of the sheltered life for women, and smiles at our English ideal of sex-equality.

Men walk alone in the streets of the cities of India. Notwithstanding, Miss Noble asserts that women have quite as much "equality" here as falls to the lot of the average single woman "living alone, or following professional careers, in the suburbs of London and other Western cities."

Self-effacement and utter unselfishness is the ideal of the devout Hindu wife and mother. Husbands and wives do not "address each other in the presence of others"; and "a wife may not name her husband, much less praise him." According to the Sister Nivedita, this reticence is based on a sense of what is called "good form" in England, and is no proof of a lack of respect for womanhood, marriage, and family life. The Indian wife adores her husband with "passionate reverence"; and in return her husband offers her boundless tenderness and protection. He was taught to honour and love his mother; he is equally reverential and affectionate towards his wife and the mother of his children. The wife is the happy, willing servitor, companion, and disciple of the husband. She kneels to him and touches his feet when he pleases her. It is not equality. "No," says Miss Noble. "But who talks of a vulgar equality, asks the Hindu wife, when she may have instead the unspeakable blessedness of offering worship?"

Do the men of India abuse this worship and the humility on the part of their wives? The author of "The Web of Indian Life" declares very insistently that they do not. A Hindu husband appears to be as admirable in the performance of all his conjugal obligations as his lovingly submissive spouse. Miss Noble reiterates again and again the blessedness of the Hindu woman's position in the home, until we are feign to believe that she is the happiest and most fortunate woman in the world.

Very little is said concerning polygamy. We read that a man may contract a second marriage if his wife remains sterile after the end of seven years, and that the first wife is by no means averse to this arrangement. Polygamy, according to Miss Noble, is rather rare in Hindu society. She has very little to say upon the question of the marriage of children to adult men.

"The courtesy of husbands to their wives is quite unfailing amongst Hindus," writes Miss Noble. "'Thou shalt not strike a woman even with a flower,' is the proverb. His wife's desire for companionship on a journey is the first claim on a man. And it is very touching to notice how, as years go on, he leans more and more to the habit of addressing her as 'O, thou mother of our son!' and presenting her to new-comers as 'my children's mother,' thus reflecting upon her his worship of motherhood."

The admiration, professed so sincerely by Miss Noble, for the marriage system of the Hindu religion is shared by an English lady known to me, who is the wife of a high-caste Hindu. She considers the unrest of the Western women who are battling so vigorously for rights, freedom, votes, and full equality with men, a tragic spectacle. English women seem to her to miss all that is best in life, all the precious things that lie within their grasp, in their eagerness to take a share in government. I cannot agree entirely with this lady. But there is a serene philosophy in her recommendation of "the sheltered life for women," which cannot be ignored.

In the West the sexes are at present torn almost to universal dissension with strife, distrust and recriminations. Apparently such antagonism is inconceivable to the mind of the loving, contented Hindu woman, who asks for nothing more than a perpetual deepening of her affection and solicitude for husband and children. She gains all by losing herself. It is nobler to serve than to lead, to heed than to teach, to obey than to command. Such is the highest ideal of the Eastern woman. "Vulgar equality" contrasted with this perfect happiness in the consciousness of the finer development of the emotions is a worthless toy. It is the woman's noblest part to give herself unselfishly and always, that her husband may love and praise her, and her children rise up and call her blessed among women.

Such self-abnegation is the keynote of Hindu feminism. How different from the cult of Western emancipation. And yet may not the West learn from the East, and the East from the West, in this vital question of the position of women? I speak as a whole-hearted supporter of the movement for the advancement of women in social life and politics.

"I desire not paradise itself if thou are not satisfied with me!" cries the divine Hindu spouse to her husband. "She is a true wife who gladdens her husband," says Raja Shekhara in the "Karpura Manjari."

I am indebted to Dr. Ananda Coomaraswamy for an excellent statement of the status of the Hindu wife, in his pamphlet, "Sati: A Vindication of the Hindu Woman," printed in 1913. The writer quotes from the "Laws of Manu," the following explicit injunction upon women:—

"Though destitute of virtue, or seeking pleasure

elsewhere, or devoid of good qualities, a husband must be constantly worshipped as a god by a faithful wife. . . . If a wife obeys her husband, she will for that reason alone be exalted in heaven."

"The production of children, the nurture of those born, and the daily life of men, of these matters woman is visibly the cause."

"She who controlling her thoughts, speech, and acts, violates not her duty to her lord, dwells with him after death in heaven, and in this world is called by the virtuous a faithful wife."

The enforcement of such reverence for husbands is quite foreign and contradictory to the conception of marriage among cultured women in the Western nations. It appears to cut at the very basis of sex-equality, and to undermine all our advanced principles of liberty for women, "freedom for wives to live their own lives," and the higher status of women generally. Dr. Coomaraswamy, anticipating this criticism, states shrewdly: "Let us at once acknowledge, with all competent observers, that the power of women over men is far greater in India than in any industrial state in the West."

This power of the Hindu women is exerted not, as in Europe, by the young and attractive, but by mothers, grandmothers and widows. Manu declares: "The mother exceedeth a thousand fathers in the right to reverence, and in the function of teacher." "I cannot emphasize too strongly," says the writer of the pamphlet, "the fact of this influence of mothers in India, not merely over children and in household matters, but over grown-up men, to whom their word is law. One might almost say that the Native States are ruled by the queen-mothers from behind the purdah."

Wherever we find goddesses in a religion, there certainly exists a higher measure of esteem for women than among the faiths honouring only male deities. Half the Hindus revere Shakti, the female symbol of deity, and they address their god as She. Shiva is a personification of the male, Uma of the female. This goddess, says Dr. Coomaraswamy, is "the ideal Hindu wife, and the first Sati, and shy beyond words; she is Shiva's humblest servant, desiring no good in heaven or earth beyond his welfare. She is in truth an image of Indian woman."

The practice of Suttee, or Sati, has puzzled and shocked the British rulers of India. We cannot understand the Hindu woman's attitude to love and marriage without a careful examination of the origin and meaning of this custom.

When Bramah died, one of his devoted wives

sacrificed herself that she might join him in heaven. Voluntarily and gladly she went to the burning pyre. This example was adopted by devout widows. Seven hundred have immolated themselves by burning, in one year, in Bengal alone.[1] They died calmly, even happily, showing extraordinary fortitude. Young wives of less than twenty years of age have relinquished life, and bade farewell to their cherished children and dearest relatives, in obedience to the overwhelming impulse of self-destruction as a noble and pious act of devotion to a husband.

English law-makers saw in this practice only the survival of "barbarism." They missed the symbolic meaning, the deep, passionate joy of the sacrifice, and the expression of a love stronger than death. Suttee was forbidden by a law of 1829; but the deep-rooted custom was not entirely abolished. The highest form of human self-sacrifice, as it is described by Sir Alfred C. Lyall, was the last custom to disappear in parts of India.

It has been supposed, quite incorrectly, that men imposed Sati upon women. The rite was introduced entirely by widows of devout faith and

[1] Hadyn "Dictionary of Dates," 5th ed. Dr. Coomaraswamy states that perhaps a thousand widows in all have committed Sati.

strong conjugal affection. Dr. Coomaraswamy traces the custom back to more than a thousand years before the Christian era, and quotes, from an old Persian author, the story of a Hindu girl who gave herself to the flames on the very day of the death of her betrothed.

Sir Frederick Halliday recounted how a widow, desiring to die by the Sati sacrifice, demonstrated to him her indifference to the agony of burning. She held her finger in a lamp "until it was burnt and twisted like a quill pen held in the flame of a candle." Sir F. Halliday, having witnessed this woman's marvellous power of endurance, felt bound to accord his permission to the petitioner to join the spirit of her dead husband.

Hinduism is the dynamic that shapes the emotion and the thought of these most feminine of women. Their crown is Love. They give life and joy.

"Conjunction with me renders life long;
[2] I give youth when I enter upon amorousness."

Buddhism, the other great ancient creed of In-

[2] "Woman is man's better half,
Woman is man's bosom friend,
Woman is redemption's source,
From woman springs the liberator."
Old Hindu Poem.

dia, has, in many of its doctrines and parables, a close similarity to the teaching of Christianity. It teaches self-renunciation, a tranquillity of the spirit, toleration, forgiveness and chastity. Gautama counsels filial respect and love of wife and child. He insists upon self-restraint and purity:—[3]

"Let the wise man avoid an unchaste life as a burning heap of coals; not being able to live a life of chastity, let him not transgress with another man's wife."

Ananda, a disciple, asks Gautama how he is to conduct himself in regard to women.

"Do not see them," is the reply.

"But if we should see them, what are we to do?"

"Abstain from speech."

"But if they should speak to us, lord, what are we to do?"

"Keep wide awake."

The Indian followers of the teaching of Zoroaster, or Zara-thustra, form a highly intellectual cult. This is the most rational of all the religions of our Indian Empire; for it is almost free from

[3] Buddhism favoured monogamy and chastity. "The percentage of illegitimate births is low in those countries where the influence of Buddhism has been greatest, and its canonical literature is chaste throughout."—T. W. Rhys David. Encyclopædia of Religion and Ethics, Vol. III., "Chastity."

myths concerning miracles, and its ethics are singularly comprehensive and liberal.

Among the Parsees, the modern exponents of the Zoroastrian philosophy, murder, infanticide, adultery,—committed by men as well as women—lying, slander, theft and perjury are condemned positively. Kindness to animals is expressly inculcated. In this faith we shall look for an ideal of equality between the sexes. And not in vain; the Parsee moral writings teach plainly that the woman is the equal of the man. The higher education of women is encouraged, and there are women doctors in the community.[4] Among Parsee women are the most zealous advocates of social and educational reforms among their sex.

The marriage customs of the Nairs of Malabar are especially interesting, as they afford an example of the persistence of the Maternal Family. Elie Reclus gives us an excellent study of these people in his "Primitive Folk." He describes the Nairs as tall, handsome, vigorous men of olive skin; they are splendid warriors, and athletes. The women are as lissome and fine-featured as the men. They have very long dark hair, which they dress with much care. Their manners are amiable.

In this community we have a curious instance of

[4] See "A Modern Zoroastrian," Samuel Laing.

polyandry and polygamy side by side. An opulent Nair is usually a polygamist; the artisans and the poor generally are polyandrists. The same system prevails in Ceylon. Among the Nairs two or three brothers marry one woman. Their sisters marry, but live afterwards as "free lances." The whole system of the sex relationship is extremely complicated; but it is a pregnant fact that the mother is strictly the head of the family.

A son living with his mother desires to possess a home of his own. As the chief of his house, he takes his sister, who is superior to his wife in domestic control. Love between the sexes is a passing matter; love between brother and sister is a deeper and enduring emotion.

Reclus states that the Brahmins tried to suppress the marriage custom of the Nairs. Nowadays the Kouline Brahmins perform for the Nair women an amorous rite, their services being in great request among the maidens of low caste. In other parts of India the priest is solicited for this consecration, notably in Burma. By this means, according to Reclus, the Brahmins hold religious sway over the Nairs, who refuse, however, to accept their political rule.

"Proud and haughty warrior though he be, the Nair cheerfully obeys his mother, assisted by his uncle, and seconded by his eldest sister; the trio manage the common property, and he who participates in it renders them an account of his exploits and achievements."[5]

The Todas of the Neilgherries practise a mixed polyandry and polygamy. "Each wife had several husbands, all brothers, and each husband several wives, all sisters. Later, three men made shift with two girls, or five with three." Polyandry appears to be waning rapidly among the Todas, and Reclus says that every well-to-do man in the tribe desires a wife of his own.

Among the Rajputs women have a notably high status. This fine race descends from early immigrants; the men are very vigorous and hardy, with handsome features, and the women are equally strong and physically beautiful.

Love among the Rajputs is an emotional and romantic passion. There is a tradition of chivalry, and men often engage in combats for the winning of brides. Masculine devotion to women is very deep and tender, and women are esteemed as almost divine.

The marriage ceremonies are simple and charming. The bride weaves garlands of flowers, which she hangs around the bridegroom's neck. Among

[5] "Primitive Folk."

the Rajputs there are marked traces of the matriarchal system. Marriage is in no sense oppressive to women, and true sex-equality seems to exist. No husband ever conducts a business or domestic affair without seeking the counsels and proposals of his wife. Undoubtedly, where men and women work side by side in common avocations, there is a high regard for the intelligence and judgment of women, as well as conjugal equality.

A testimony as to the power of the mothers in India is given by Father Elwin,[6] a missionary. He says that mothers of families direct the religious beliefs of their children, and rule in all matters over even their grown-up sons.

If the condition of the wife under Hinduism is inferior to that of married women under Christianity, which has been questioned by some English writers, her status as a mother is one of supreme authority. Throughout the Indian Empire, the mother is the practical, actual head of the family.

[6] "Fifty-four Years in Poona City."

CHAPTER VI

THE CULT OF WOMAN AND LOVE

SAKTI, the female deity, is Woman and Love, and Motherhood. She is worshipped by the intellectual class, the scribes and the clerks. Sakti is the men's goddess among a numerous following. There are holy rites of a sexual character associated with her adoration. The word *sakti* signifies power and energy.

As I have said before, where women are exalted as the goddesses of religion, they usually occupy a higher status than among the worshippers of male deities. In India, therefore, notwithstanding the much-assailed institution of the zenana, women are by no means the vassals or the mere chattels of men, as we are sometimes taught to believe.

"Far from India's being the land of the uniform oppression of women," writes Miss Margaret Noble, "by a uniform method, it represents the whole cycle of feminist institutions. There is literally no theory of feminine rights and position that does not find illustration somewhere within her boundaries."

The erotic valuation of women in India is not,

as it may appear at first, a simple expression of sensuousness. It is something deeper, more subtle. Love and religion are intermingled, even in the zenana.

The amours of Krishna and Radha, in the "Prem-Sagar," are said by some Occidental critics to bore with their reiterations of love-adventures, and have been described as "indecent." Probably, judged from the prurient-prudish standpoint of the West, they are so. But who shall decide? Does not the Old Testament, used in our churches, contain the most amorous of pictures in the "Song" ascribed to King Solomon?

The veil screening the face of Hindu women has been accepted as an emblem of the oppression of the sex. May it not possess a very different significance? It is true that a woman may not show her face to any man save father, brother, and husband. But the veil is, in a sense, a tribute to Woman, whose loveliness and sweetness of countenance has in it something sacred, which must not be exposed to the common gaze. No Hindu woman feels herself degraded by the practice of veiling part of her features. She would be insulted if you suggested that the veil symbolised her bondage to men.

The life behind the purdah, the thick curtain that conceals the women of the zenana from the gaze of strangers, seems to Western eyes oppressive, even degrading. A man-doctor, who calls professionally upon a lady of the zenana, feels her pulse and questions her through the curtain.

Is this imprisonment? Indian women in the mass do not think so. The rights to which religion and law entitle them are accorded duly behind the purdah. They are queens of the home, not active competitors with men in the scramble for existence. Their greatest ambition is to be *women,* and that ideal connotes much that the woman of the West is discarding in scornful rebellion. Spinsterhood, and "the right to live one's own life," —the supreme consummation of a large number of revolutionary British women—make no appeal to an Indian woman. Her strongest impulses are to fulfil her womanhood, to experience love, and to bear children. That is her vocation, her ambition, and her joy.

I have repeated the testimony of English women, who discern, in the home-life of India, a perfect adjustment of the functions and responsibilities of both sexes. But there are critics, Indian as well as foreign; and we must listen to them. It is, of course, incredible that there are no malcontents among the Hindu women.

The wave of feminine revolt is sweeping steadily

eastwards. It has reached Turkey, and has spread to the farther East. In another chapter I shall present a very different point of view from those of certain of my Indian friends and correspondents.

For the present, we are considering the Hindu reverence for woman as the lover, the bride, the lifegiver. She is more than this. There is a sacredness, something that arouses awe, in her body, and her physical functions. To show how deep and sincere is this mingled emotion of piety and sex-love, I cannot do better than quote some lines by the greatest living Indian poet, Rabindra Nath Tagore, the winner of the Nobel Prize for Literature in 1913.

GOD AND THE ASCETIC

At midnight the would-be ascetic announced:
"This is the time to give up my home and seek for God. Ah! who has held me so long in delusion here?"
God whispered, "I!" But the ears of the man were stopped.
With a baby asleep at her breast lay his wife, peacefully sleeping on one side of the bed.
The man said: "Who are ye that have fooled me so long?"
The voice said again, "They are God!" But he heard it not.
The baby cried out in its dream, nestling close to its mother.
God commanded, "Stop, fool; leave not thy home." But still he heard not.
God sighed and complained, "Why does My servant wander to seek Me, forsaking Me?"

How exquisitely the writer expresses the holiness of love and parentage.

Here is a beautiful tribute to a woman from her lover:—

HALF WOMAN AND HALF DREAM

O, woman, you are not merely the handiwork of God, but also of men; these are ever endowing you with beauty from their hearts.

Poets are weaving for you a web with threads of golden imagery; painters are giving your form ever new immortality.

The sea gives its pearls, the mines their gold, the summer gardens their flowers to deck you, to cover you, to make you more precious.

The desire of men's hearts has shed its glory over your youth.

You are one half woman and one half dream.

And here, too, is the purest expression of passion from the lips of a woman:—

TELL ME, MY LOVER

Tell me if this be all true, my lover, tell me if this be true:

Is it true that my lips are sweet, like the opening bud of the first conscious love?

Do the memories of vanished months of May linger in my limbs?

Is it true, is it true, that your love travelled alone through ages and worlds in search of me?

That when you found me at last your age-long desire found utter peace in my gentle speech and my eyes and lips and flowing hair?

Is it then true that the mystery of the infinite is written on this little forehead of mine?

Tell me, my lover, if all this be true.

The sanctity of sex is unfortunately a phrase almost without meaning in the Western world, where physical passion is often dismissed as "mere animality." Ages ago, the Oriental peoples recognised that the highest sexual morality is only compatible with grave and frank acceptance of the methods ordained by the gods for the propagation of the human species. The Christian has rarely indeed accepted the Almighty's plan in the same reverential spirit. How revolting are the conceptions of St. Bernard and most of the Fathers: "You have never seen a viler dunghill!" (*i.e.,* than the human body) cries St. Bernard. How contemptuous and coarse is St. Odo's estimate of woman. Among the few early Christian teachers who showed sanity in this respect was Clement of Alexandria, who declared: "We should not be ashamed to name what God has not been ashamed to create." [1]

Such contempt for the body, and for the supreme function of procreation, would be deemed the gravest blasphemy by all devout Hindus and Mohammedans. "It seems never to have entered the heads of the Hindu legislators," said Sir William Jones ("Works," Vol. II., p. 311), "that anything

[1] See "Studies in the Psychology of Sex," Vol. VI., Havelock Ellis.

natural could be offensively obscene, a singularity which pervades all their writings, but is no proof of the depravity of their morals."

R. Schmidt, writing on "Indian Erotics," in German, says: "Love in India, both as regards theory and practice, possesses an importance which it is impossible for us even to conceive." Quite so; the Western point of view is either prudish or prurient, usually a mixture of both.

There cannot be the least doubt, when sexual love is rightly appraised and respected as a part of the scheme of a divine ruler, or of beneficent Nature, that the relations of men and women are set upon a higher psychic level, than when passion is associated with uncleanness. Hindu culture recognised this in the earliest days. Chastity, purity, restraint, were inculcated, and periods of ascetic living were commended as beneficial discipline. But there was no shirking of the great vital questions of sex, and no abuse of processes designed by the gods.

Much of the conjugal serenity and happiness of the East is due to the heed devoted by husbands to an understanding of sex-love and the psychology of woman. Whether we approve polygamy, or denounce the practice, the truth remains that the men of the East are beloved by their wives, and that married discord is far less frequent than in the West. It is easy to attribute this fact to the subservience of women. We have seen that such subservience is far more apparent than actual. There is hardly a hint of it in the modern Hindu love-poetry.

The point to observe is that the Hindus do not contemn any phase of the impulse that unites man to woman. They cannot jeer at love, for the whole of their religious traditions forbid such profanity. To make lovers and love-making a subject for jesting is impossible.

In the "Seven Hundred Maxims of Hâla" are some passages revealing the fervid and passionate nature of early Hindu love:—

"He sees nothing but her face, and she, too, is quite intoxicated by his looks. Both, satisfied with each other, act as if in the whole world there were no other woman or man."

The following maxim treats of the evanescent quality of passion:—

"Love departs when lovers are separated; it departs when they see too much of each other; it departs in consequence of malicious gossip; aye, it departs also without these causes."

On the beauty of women Hindu poets are eloquent. The Lotus Woman, the embodiment of the perfect physical ideal of feminine loveliness, is thus described in "The Kama Sutra":—

> "She in whom the following signs and symptoms appear is called a Padmini: Her face is pleasing as the full moon, her body, well clothed with flesh, is as soft as Shiras or mustard flower; her skin is fine, tender, fair as the gum or lotus, never dark coloured. Her eyes are bright and beautiful as the orbs of the fawn, well cut and with reddish corners. Her bosom is hard, full, and high; she has a good neck; her nose is straight and lovely. . . . She walks with swan-like (more exactly flamingo-like) gait, and her voice is low and musical as the note of the Kokila bird (the Indian cuckoo). She delights in white raiment, in fine jewels, and in rich dresses. She eats little, sleeps lightly, and being as respectful and religious as she is clever and courteous, she is ever anxious to worship the gods, and to enjoy the conversation of Brahmans. Such, then, is the Padmini, or lotus-woman."

The Hindu woman is usually short, and slight in build. Her complexion is a dark brown. In Kashmir, the women are taller, and some have lighter complexions. The most statuesque forms among the women of India are said to be seen in Kashmir.

In most parts the married women have the red *Kum-Kum* mark painted upon the forehead.

The veil is worn in the North of India, but seldom among the women of the South. Most of the zenanas are in Bengal, Sind, Punjâb, and the North generally.

In Ceylon, the women most loved for their charms have long plentiful hair, blue eyes, and curved eyebrows. The lips should be red, the teeth small. Her breasts must be small and firm; the hips wide, the limbs tapering, and the skin of the body delicate.[2]

This adoration of the beautiful features and forms of women is of religious significance in the East. Instead of the dread, and frequently the repulsion, from feminine grace and loveliness, so often expressed by the early Christian writers, the Hindus personify Woman as Beauty. Such worship is not simply the outcome of sexual desire. It is also a poetical, æsthetic valuation of the human body. It is the artist's loving appreciation of the form of man and woman, the spirit that animates Rodin when he confesses that, in his eyes, all women are beautiful.

It is true that woman makes a strong sensuous appeal to the Hindu, which he never conceals. But we must remember that "the sensual East" is also the home of the sternest renunciations of carnal pleasures, the strictest asceticism, the most severe penances and self-martyrdom ever known among humankind. No Western saint ever endured as much for the welfare of his soul as the

[2] "An Account of the Interior of Ceylon"—Davy.

self-imposed torments of the Eastern priests, fakirs, and holy men, and women, in the suppression of desire.

It is the white man who is accountable for the introduction of sexual vices unknown, or rarely practised, in the East before his coming. He has brought venereal disease, and implanted its mortal poisons in the blood of thousands of healthy primitive people. He has taught unclean vulgarity of thought and speech to innocent natives free from its taint. He has introduced intoxicating spirits, and encouraged their use among sober savages. Let the white man pause before he speaks in condemnation of "the abominable sexual practices" of the Orient.

One of the best-informed and most sympathetic writers upon Indian life is Mrs. Flora Annie Steel. This lady lived for many years in the East, and her volume "India" and her novels show how closely she has observed the people. Mrs. Steel's testimony, while it lacks the high enthusiasm of Miss Margaret Noble, is still very favourable concerning the position of Hindu women. She has the cosmopolitan, rather than the average Anglo-Indian, outlook. After a diligent reading of this author's chapter on Indian women, and other parts of her book, one is almost compelled to assent to

Miss Noble's view; for very much that Mrs. Steel writes supports her compatriot's optimistic vision of Hindu life.

Mrs. Steel says shrewdly that, though the monopoly of a man by his wife, as in Western marriage, is unknown in India, the sons are invariably monopolised by the mothers. The maternal authority is unquestionable and autocratic. In the East generally, women are despotic over the men.[3] Nowhere are men so henpecked as in India. Wife-beating is extremely rare, in spite of the assertiveness of the wives. There seems little doubt that the Hindu husband is conspicuous for his docility and patience. There are "few happier households than Indian ones," says Mrs. Steel. Among the Jat and Sikh villagers a charming *camaraderie* prevails between men and women. This is often the case where the sexes work side by side on an equality.

Unkindness to children is hardly known. We shall note that this virtue of parental love is almost universal in Eastern countries. Divorce is practically unknown. To the Hindus marriage is a grave and sacred union. In wedlock the husband is "a perfect prey to his womenfolk, at any rate for some years." Surely this statement

[3] *Op. cit.* Mrs. Steel.

should be considered by the critics of Indian marriage before they lament "the degraded position of our Indian sisters."

"We in the West," writes Mrs. Steel, "are talking of discarding marriage, but played in Eastern fashion marriage has guarded much that woman holds most dear."

Even the missionaries are bound to acknowledge that sexual morality is high in India. Mrs. Steel asserts that the standard of national morality is "far higher in India than it is in England." In Persia and in India the code of sex morals in ancient times was almost cruel in its severity. The tradition still lives. It is true that mercenary commerce of the sexes is practised in the towns, but in a far less flagrant and callous manner than in the Western civilisations. Seduction is a very serious offence in India, and the betrayed girl is always acutely distressed. There is, however, proper provision for the few children born out of marriage.

In the light of the careful evidence of such an authority as Mrs. Steel, it is time for us to recognize that all the sexual virtues are not restricted to the West. It is to be regretted that missionary zeal has fostered the view in England that the women in India are merely the serfs of sensual, tyrannous men. As Mrs. Steel remarks, we have been told by the ordinary Anglo-Indian and the missionaries that India is "thoroughly degraded, hopelessly, helplessly depraved, and utterly enslaved." Yet, in spite of polygamy, the Hindu woman's position compares very favourably with that of her Western sisters.

Mrs. Steel would perhaps go further than this. The following extract is from a lecture delivered by her:—

"In an original address on 'The Women of India,' at the Manor House Club, Bredon's Norton, yesterday, Mrs. Steel championed the superior domestic position of the Indian woman as against the European woman.

"According to Mrs. Steel the Eastern wife has a very easy time of it. She does not have to rise to prepare her husband's breakfast or that of her children, for the simple reason that having supped plentifully they do not require any breakfast beyond a chunk of food, to which they help themselves. And so throughout the day the Indian woman's domestic duties are of the lightest. There are no rooms crowded with furniture to sweep and dust, and not even a bed to make, while the clothing for the family is too simple to burden the housewife.

"Touching upon the problems of wifehood and motherhood, Mrs. Steel made the bold statement that during her long residence in India she had not seen as much matrimonial unhappiness, even taking polygamy into account, as she had witnessed in our own land."—*Daily Chronicle.*

I have cited passages from the Hindu sacred books and the ancient codes showing that the rights of women were not disregarded in India. The following passage is from the "Rigveda":—

"Though the wife, like the children, was subject to the will of her husband, her position was one of greater honour in the Rigvedic age than later, for she shared with her husband the performance of sacrifice. She was mistress of the house, with control not only over servants and slaves but also over the unmarried brothers and sisters of her husband. As the family could only be continued in the male line, prayers for abundance of sons are very frequent. But the birth of daughters is never desired in the *Rigveda;* it is deprecated in the *Atharvaveda;* the *Yajurveda* refers to girls being exposed when born; and one of the Brahmanas observes that 'to have a daughter is a misery.' This prejudice survives in India to the present day with unabated force."[4]

Gyanendra Kumar Ray Chaudhuri, writing on "Hindu Love," says:—

"The primitive civilization and crude morality of the less advanced and educated Hindu are far better than any form of Western civilization. There is much in the East which the West should do well to adopt. Among the Hindus conjugal union is a thing to be kept inviolate as a sacred tie not to be dissolved even by death. The so-called emancipated and enlightened females should learn from their benighted sisters how

[4] "Imp. Gazetteer of India," 1908.

sacred the relation is between husband and wife. In the estimation of the Hindu female it is invested with a heavenly grandeur which passes all description."

The same author writes of Hindu women:—

"Their chastity, their devotion, their love, are admired by all sensible men."

Many of the Hindu classic poets and romance writers extol passionate love, and marriage for love alone, which proves that, in the old days, more freedom of choice was permitted to lovers.

CHAPTER VII

THE ZENANA

THE princely harems of India rival in magnificence those of Egypt and Turkey.[1] When an ex-king of Oude was awarded a mighty revenue from his kingdom, as a pension from the English, he built a miniature walled city on the Hooghly. Here he ruled over several thousand subjects, and held a stately court. His chief wives were two in number, and he had thirty-nine inferior wives, called Mahuls, "bearers of children." Besides these women, the ex-sovereign owned one hundred Begums. His family consisted of thirty-one sons and twenty-five daughters; fifty-six children, and all of them living.

This potentate's stipend of £10,000 a month was inadequate. He was always in debt. His palaces were from three to four, and he occupied them alternately. Surrounding the royal residences was one of the finest menageries in the world. There were "20,000 birds, beasts and snakes," and in the tank were numerous kinds of fish. The pigeons

[1] The term zenana is derived from the Persian zan, meaning woman.

alone numbered 18,000. The monarch who presided here, like Solomon in all his glory, had artistic taste. He painted pictures and composed songs for the nautch girls, who sang them in all parts of India. He had a troupe of dancers, and an orchestra of musicians. Such was the splendour of this deposed king's harem and estates, in 1874, as described by Mr. James Routledge, in his volume on "English Rule and Native Opinion in India."

"And all this House of love was peopled fair
With sweet attendance, so that in each part
With lovely sights were gentle faces found,
Soft speech and willing service; each one glad
To gladden, pleased at pleasure, proud to obey;
Till life glided beguiled, like a smooth stream.

* * * * * *

"And night and day served there a chosen band
Of nautch-girls, cup-bearers, and cymballers,
Delicate, dark-browed ministers of love,
Who fanned the sleeping eyes of the happy Prince,
And when he waked, led back his thoughts to bliss
With music whispering through the blooms, and charm
Of amorous songs and dreamy dances, linked
By chime of ankle-bells and wave of arms
And silver-vina-strings; while essences
Of musk and champak, and the blue haze spread
[2] From burning spices, soothed his soul again."

The "sheltered life," so enthusiastically com-

[2] "The Light of Asia."—Sir Edwin Arnold.

mended by my lady friend, is, of course, very alluring to many women when lived under such luxurious conditions as those related in Sir Edwin Arnold's poem. Numbers of women in the West would enjoy this indolent, secure, and voluptuous existence.

As a matter of fact, there are American women living in Indian zenanas. They have renounced the Christian faith, embraced Hinduism, and become entirely Oriental in their lives and practices. I know an English professional dancer, who informed me that several friends, in her profession, have entered Turkish harems. One of these girls describes the life as "delightful." She is richly fed, beautifully dressed, and has an ample income and her own apartments. This immunity from the strife of maintaining life appeals powerfully to women of a fairly numerous class. They desire neither "economic independence," nor "emancipation." In the West they marry for comfort and ease; in the East they welcome the chance of entering the harem.

Let us understand quite clearly that polygamous marriage in the Indian Empire is chiefly the practice of the influential and wealthy classes, and that it is far from general, even amongst the rich Mohammedans and Brahmins. The *soudras* (working class of low castes) and the poorer folk are almost entirely monogamous. But it is a monogamy differing essentially from that of Christian countries.

The legal and religious single marriage of England is an enduring link that can only be severed by divorce. Legal separation is an incomplete dissolution, inasmuch as the sundered persons cannot enter into marriage. In Catholic nations the tie is still more difficult to loosen. In India divorce is easy. You may, if you choose, engage in a succession of monogamous unions, without forfeiting social esteem, or infringing the principles of your creed.

Facility of divorce does not tend naturally to inconstancy, in spite of all that is said to the contrary by those who oppose it. In Burma, for example, divorce is a simple and speedy process; but such separation between the married is rare. There is a reason for this comparative rarity of divorce in the East, and especially among the upper classes. When a man has four legal wives, and a number of secondary spouses, entirely at his disposal, he is apt to overlook, or to deal leniently, with the faults of one of his chief wives.

A discontented husband, under the monogamic sway, sometimes seeks love, or the gratification of sexual passion, outside of the home. Often he maintains a second house, and lives a double life, or he frequents the company of *demi-mondaines.* There is a high scarcity value in sex in the West. This is almost unknown in the East, where everyone is enjoined to marry. If one wife in the harem is fractious and unmanageable, there are three others who may be amiable and amenable. There is no strong incentive to wander. Besides, has not a rajah a troupe of dancing girls and slaves as well? All of these dependents are at his command.

The Eastern servant has no higher ambition than to become an *ikbal,* or favourite, of her master. She ceases then to be a serf; she has a status, rights, and property of her own. When she bears a child, she is for ever a free woman. She can enforce her master to maintain her and the children. If she becomes a wife, and the husband desires to disavow her, he is bound to make her a substantial allowance for life.

Divorce may be easy, but responsibility does not end with mere repudiation of a wife. It is a tax upon a rajah's income when he has to support a number of divorced wives and their families. Therefore, though total separation is apparently facile under polygamy, it is not quite so simple as it seems at first glance.

In a case of dissolution of marriage, a man must prove that his wife has been guilty of one or more of the following offences: Adultery, disobedience, bad temper. Ill health is a cause for divorce, and so is barrenness. If a woman gives birth only to female infants during ten years, the husband may discharge her. But on whatever pretext, and through whatever fault, a woman is divorced, she has always a claim for proper maintenance.

In the ancient days in India, plurality of wives was far commoner than at the present time. Among the Hindu religionists it is not usual to find two women living as the wives of one man. The people of India are not generally polygamous in the strict sense. Polygamy is the privilege of the rich, but many of the wealthy are married to only one wife. This fact must be recognised, for there are people in Great Britain and America who refer to the polygamy of Indians as though the whole nation practised this form of marriage.

Polygamy is allowed by religion, law, and public opinion. The great Dasaratha, the father of Rama, was said to own 60,000 women. Kings, princes, and noble personages used to maintain large harems. Every woman, from the favourite wife to the lowest slave-girl, might be the sexual consort of her lord if he so desired. There was the fullest outlet for the variety impulse of affluent men.

Sivaji, the Maharajah, married as many as eighteen women in a single day. This was, however, due to a curious error. The ruler wished a wife for himself, and partners for some of his courtiers. A number of beautiful maidens were selected, and brought to the palace under the misapprehension that they were all destined to share the great man's favour. Upon discovering their mistake, the girls broke into lamentations and displayed the utmost disappointment. Sivaji, being a chivalrous and kindly man, thereupon determined to marry the whole bevy of virgins.

An understanding of the Indian character is impossible unless we appreciate the great importance that eroticism plays in the life of the East. In England the average man, and the great mass of women, fear voluptuousness almost as they fear sin. Climate has some influence in this alleged indifference to sensual pleasure; but religion and tradition have probably a much weightier sway. We know perfectly well that almost every conceivable form of gross sensuality is practised among the Northern and the Western races. But we lift our eyes piously, and affect horror at legalised polygamy, a time-honoured religious form of marriage in the

East, permitted by a noble reformer, the Prophet Mohammed, and by the great spiritual teachers of Hinduism.

Uncontrolled indulgence is without question disastrous to the individual and the race. Let us not, however, fall into the error of assuming that the Oriental attitude towards sex, with its frankness, and joyous acceptation of all that is good in the physical expression of love, is of the same quality as the cold lasciviousness and obscenity that so often distinguishes Teutonic and Anglo-Saxon ideas of sexual passion.

Phallicism reverenced sex as a symbol of the whole of life, of increase, and of good. To-day men mock ignorantly at the images and signs of this ancient cult. There is a deplorable tendency to confuse beautiful symbols with the vulgar pornography of corrupt modern cities. Such vulgarity is foreign to the Eastern mind. Freedom of conversation does not necessarily spell indecency, though imperfectly educated people in the West seem to think so. Christianity, as expounded by the Fathers and the ascetic saints, besmirched love and sex so completely and ruthlessly that we have never succeeded in cleansing our thoughts upon the great and solemn motor-force of the world.

The Oriental may be in some cases too much preoccupied with the physical phases of sex-love. At all events, his preoccupation is open and avowed, and not concealed, and hypocritically denied. Behind all this interest in love, there is a deep esteem for the procreative power, whence springs most, if not indeed all, of the nobler human aspirations and virtues.

What may be called justly a sanction for a cultivated eroticism is to be found in the religious creeds of the Eastern world.

Hindu sacred writings do not leave out of account the relations of the sexes. They contain explicit teaching upon the bodily conjugal rites, often expressed in beautiful and reverential phrases. Nothing could be purer, more lofty and poetical, than some of the counsels to husbands and wives, to fathers and mothers. Several writers on Indian life refer to "indecent pictures" on the walls of temples. One of these observers is, however, bound to admit that the paintings are "not licentious." The average traveller does not stay to inquire into the symbolism of such pictures. He immediately associates them with Western ideas of propriety and concludes that their sole purpose is to amuse or to shock. This is a very ignorant appraisement. It recalls the furtive chuckle of a lout in the contemplation of a superb painting of a nude figure in one of our public museums.

Polygamy is closely connected with the sacred erotic conceptions of the Eastern mind. Woman in India is beloved and desired, as she is in England, for her physical grace and loveliness, as well as for her virtue, sweetness, and gentleness of heart. She is a symbol, a principle, a half-divine being. There is magic in her. Endless are the taboos surrounding her sex. The curse of a woman is terrible. Her kiss is a benediction to the warrior. She is exalted as a goddess. As Sakti, representing the female principle, she is deeply revered and loved.

These facts should cause us to reconsider all our preconceived notions about "the degradation of the Eastern woman." Let us try earnestly to comprehend the Hindu point of view regarding women. In all parts of the world woman stands for the Incomprehensible, the mysterious. "Souvent femme varie" has given rise to a fervent, bewildered, masculine attention. The Hindus, perhaps more than any other race, have shown a great curiosity and awe concerning the female sex. Woman is highly susceptible to religious ecstasy. She is a stoical martyr under such stimulus. Her nervous organisation and her sex function cause weird manifestations.

Under certain conditions her touch is baneful; at others it is beneficent. According to a primitive legend woman was stung by a snake, and has never recovered from the sting. Maternity invested her with something mysterious, which must be deeply respected. In ancient times, she was the most fitting of human sacrifices to the gods.

CHAPTER VIII

HINDU WOMEN AND THE SACRED BOOKS

THE position of women in all countries is largely determined by the teaching of the prevailing faith. In the monogamous Christian nations, the social and marital status of women is due chiefly to the precepts of St. Paul and the ascetic Fathers. Hindu women owe their position principally to the elaborate counsels and rules laid down by Vishnu and Manu. Indian sacred writings abound with the most explicit commands upon the relations of the sexes.

Manu fears woman as all men fear an overwhelming fascination. He desires that she should be justly and kindly treated. The necessity for her protection is constantly urged upon men. "Dependence" is a word that arouses revolt in the breasts of those earnest European claimants for women's rights, who write, and lecture, and agitate. But the Hindu woman likes to be protected.

Thus speaks Manu:—

"Day and night women must be kept in dependence by the males of their families, and if they attach themselves to sensual enjoyments, they must be kept under control."

"Her father protects her in childhood, her husband protects her in youth, and her sons protect her in old age. A woman is never fit for independence."

"He who carefully guards his wife, preserves the purity of his offspring, virtuous conduct, his family, himself, and his means of acquiring merit."

"No man can completely guard women by force; but they can be guarded by the employment of the following expedients: Let the husband employ his wife in the collection and expenditure of his wealth, in keeping everything clean, in the fulfilment of religious duties, in the preparation of his food, and in looking after the household utensils."

"Drinking spirituous liquor, associating with wicked people, separation from husband, rambling abroad, sleeping at unseasonable hours, and dwelling in other men's houses, are the six causes of the ruin of women."

"When creating them Manu allotted to women a love of their bed, of their seat, and of ornament, impure desires, wrath, dishonesty, malice, and bad conduct."

The following laws relate to the separation of the married:—

"For one year let a husband bear with a wife who hates him, but after the lapse of a year let him deprive her of her property and cease to cohabit with her."

"She who shows disrespect to a husband, who is addicted to some evil passion, is a drunkard, or diseased, shall be deserted for three months and be deprived of her ornaments and furniture."

"But she who shows aversion towards a mad or outcast husband, a eunuch, one destitute of manly strength, or one afflicted with such disease as punish crimes, shall neither be cast off nor be deprived of her property."

In "The Institutes of Vishnu" there are a number of clauses relating to marriage. A man is forbidden to marry a woman of a lower caste. No woman having six fingers can be married, nor one having lost one of her limbs.

There is a curious prohibition against marriage with a woman of decidedly red hair. Light, or golden, hair is, of course, extremely uncommon among the dark-skinned races. The blonde is not fitted to survive in very hot countries, nor, it is said, in highly-civilised states. A distrust of persons with red hair is fairly common in many countries. Certain specific physiological, moral, and mental characteristics are supposed to accompany red hair. Generally-speaking, red hair is not admired by the uneducated classes, but it is sometimes highly attractive to men of the artistic type.

It would seem, from the proscription against marrying red-haired women, that an ancient prejudice existed in India regarding the hair so much admired by many of the old Italian painters.

The Hindu prefers the woman "robed in the long night of her deep hair." He looks upon red hair as abnormal among the women of his race, and the abnormal is often dreaded and disliked in other countries besides India. As the Hindus admire soft and silky hair, we can, in part, trace here the prejudice against auburn hair, which is usually dry and coarse to the touch.

Finally, Vishnu forbids marriage with a woman who "talks idly."

The stigma of virginity must be removed as soon as possible after a girl attains to the function of womanhood. If no man chooses her within three months, she is at liberty to make her choice.

We will now survey some of "The Duties of a Woman," according to Vishnu.

To live in harmony with her husband.

To show reverence (by embracing their feet and such-like attentions) to her mother-in-law, father-in-law, to Gurus (such as elders), to divinities, and to guests.

To keep household articles (such as the winnowing basket and the rest) in good array.

To maintain saving habits.

To be careful with her pestle and mortar and other domestic utensils.

Not to practise incantations with roots, or other kinds of witchcraft.

To observe auspicious customs.

Not to decorate herself with ornaments, or to partake of amusements, while her husband is absent from home.

Not to resort to the houses of strangers during the absence of her husband.

Not to stand near the doorway or by the windows of her house.

Not to act by herself in any matter.

To remain subject, in her infancy, to her father; in her

youth to her husband; and in her old age to her sons. After the death of her husband to preserve her chastity, or to ascend the pile after him.

No sacrifice, no penance, and no feasting allowed to women apart from their husbands; to pay obedience to her lord is the only means for a woman to obtain bliss in heaven.

A woman who keeps a fast or performs a penance in the lifetime of her lord, deprives her husband of his life, and will go to hell.

The following advice to would-be husbands is from the "Upanishads."

"She is the best of women whose garments are pure. Therefore let him approach a woman whose garments are pure, and whose fame is pure, and address her."

"If she do not give in, let him, as he likes, bribe her with presents. And if she then do not give in, let him, as he likes, beat her with a stick, or with his hand overcome her, saying: 'With my manly strength and glory I take away thy glory,' and thus she becomes unglorious."

"If she gives in, he says: 'With manly strength and glory I give thee glory,' and then they both become glorious."

Are these ordinances obeyed to the letter? We may decide that some laxity is as permissible to the Hindu woman who reads Vishnu's "Institutes," as to her British sister who is acquainted with the Pauline Epistles. It is fairly evident, from all that we hear of the present position of the women of India, that neither Manu or Vishnu are invariably accepted quite literally.

In most of the extracts that I have given, from

the "Laws of Manu" and "The Institutes of Vishnu," the bias seems undoubtedly to the advantage of men. But elsewhere in these pages I have quoted passages from Hindu literature which reveal rather less of the patriarchal spirit. And I am sure that Dr. Coomaraswamy would tell me that no clause in these codes militates directly against the highest interests of women.

Woman everywhere, even in polyandrous tribes, is a subject of inhibitions, restrictions, and customs arising from her sex and her great office as mother. In England, as Tennyson wrote, she is "cramped under worse than South Sea isle taboo." Is woman more "cramped" in our Indian Empire? The answer must be that, in some respects, women enjoy a better social and family standing in India than they do amongst ourselves.

"Seclusion," which is so repugnant to the Western woman's mind, is very different from the isolation of women in England. It is a seclusion in an atmosphere of love, conjugal and parental. The lot of the English single woman is frequently one of loveless seclusion. Numberless are the unmarried women of our own country who live in unavowed revolt against the deprivation of love. For every Hindu woman there is a husband, and, in most marriages, a strong and abiding love.

CHAPTER IX

THE DISABILITIES OF INDIAN WOMEN

A DISTINGUISHED Indian poetess, Mrs. Sarojini Naidu, who is in England while I write these lines, is known amongst us as an ardent pioneer of a women's movement in her own country. This cultured lady has written two volumes of poems, in the English language, entitled "The Golden Threshold" and "The Bird of Time." She is an eloquent public speaker, temperate, earnest, and thoughtful.

Mrs. Naidu says that "Indian womanhood is feeling, as it were, the ripple of the world movement, and it awakes noble echoes from the past." This writer thinks that Hindu women have lost a glorious past inheritance: "Ours is an absolutely unbroken tradition, overlaid and obscured, but still so real that it has prevented the raising of anything like the sex-barrier I find in England. We are not pioneers, but reawakeners."

Mrs. Naidu's ideal of freedom for women is not the winning of political powers through the franchise, but "a social and intellectual existence, equal to, while different from, that of men." She states that educated men in India, both Hindus and Mohammedans, are giving attentive heed to the claims of women.

In the "Laws of Manu," the "Maxims of Hâla," and in other Indian writings, sacred and secular, we discover here and there a foreshadowing of the modern ideal of romantic love. Accretions in belief and doctrine, and probably the introduction of polygamy, the immolation of widows, and the precedence given to sons before daughters, obscured much of this ancient Aryan idealism, and weakened the position of women. More submission was inculcated to women; there arose practices that give evidence of a growth of the patriarchal system in family life, with a lessening of women's liberty and opportunity for freedom of social companionship with men.

Miss Margaret Noble and Dr. Ananda Coomaraswamy, whose opinions I have quoted, uphold, with fervour and admiration, the caste system, and practically the whole of Hindu customs relating to marriage and women. There are institutions to which they scarcely allude. They are naturally anxious to prove a case, and I must admit that, to a great extent, they succeed in their object.

Yet if we turn to the Pundita Ramabai Sarasvati

for enlightenment as to the condition of women in India, we shall learn that there are flagrant imperfections in the marriage laws. This Indian lady has drawn up an indictment in a little volume, called "The High Caste Hindu Woman." Her criticism deserves our attention as representing at any rate the earnest opinions of an educated native woman, who desires the highest well-being for her sisters.

One of the wrongs of women in India, whether living in monogamous marriage or in the zenana, lies in the disability of the mother who bears only daughters. We have been assured that India is a country where women are held in the highest esteem. How is it, then, that the female infant is unwelcomed by the fathers? Surely, in a society that reveres womanhood and maternity, the potential mother should be almost sacred.

According to the Pundita Sarasvati such respect for the girl-baby is never expressed. On the contrary, there are many mothers who look upon the birth of a girl as a great calamity. Such a misfortune is a source of the keenest chagrin in the father, who is apparently moved to resentment against the mother.

The Hindu wife who has brought a son into existence is regarded with the husband's favour, while she who produces a daughter appears to earn his reprobation. So powerful is the longing for male children that Hindu women employ many spells in the hope of conceiving sons. The son-giving gods are invoked with an anxious fervour. Is it not possible that this anxiety in the mind of a pregnant woman may have an injurious influence on her offspring? I know that this is a subject of controversy. But it seems to me that such solicitude cannot fail to affect the health of the mother, and that her state may react upon the unborn child.

The unwanted daughter in India is an object for pity. She is even in some families upbraided by her parents for being a girl. A wife, asked if she has children, will reply, "I have nothing"; and "nothing" means a girl. The Pundita, whom I am quoting, describes the lives of many girls as terribly unhappy through the stigma of their sex. She says that brothers frequently despise their sisters.

The Hindu Scriptures, like the Christian Bible, contain statements that often appear highly contradictory. We have read passages from the sacred books of India extolling women and the mother. But the "Laws of Manu" contain this sentence: "Of dishonour woman is the cause; of enmity woman is the cause; of mundane existence woman is the cause; hence woman is to be avoided."

Again, in a Hindu proverb, we read:—

"Woman is a great whirlpool of suspicion; a dwelling place of vices; full of deceits; a hindrance in the way of heaven; the gate of hell."

This likening of woman to the "gate of hell" recalls some of the denunciations of the Christian Fathers of a much later date.

Being born a girl is almost a misdemeanour. The penalty overshadows and darkens the whole life until, perchance, redemption comes with the birth of a son. We begin to understand why infanticide was formerly so common in India, and why it still survives in some parts of the country. One writer says that Hindu women often threw their female children into the river, to preserve them from the hard fate awaiting them in life.

Barrenness is a grievous trial to a Hindu woman, imposing very serious social disabilities, including divorce. Numberless are the invocations, the spells, the incantations, and the mystical devices resorted to by women of the East as a cure for sterility. So great is the dread of infecundity that, throughout the Orient, women, whether married or single, adopt the most extravagant methods to ensure child-bearing.

Mr. E. S. Hartland, in his excellent and thorough investigation of "Primitive Paternity," has gathered together a number of the practices of Indian women. In Bombay a sterile woman will cut off a piece of the end of a robe of a fruitful woman as an amulet; or she will "steal a new-born infant's shirt, steep one end of it in water, drink the water, and destroy the shirt. The child to whom the clothing belonged would then die and be born again from the womb of the woman performing the ceremony."

Embracing the image of the god representing fertility, a very old and common custom, is still practised by women in India. All over the country there are figures, and even unshaped stones, alleged to impart fruitfulness to women.

The yearning for male children induces Hindu women to perform several ceremonies. In the third month of pregnancy, according to the Grikya-Sûtvas, the husband who desires a son should administer to his wife curds from a cow, which has a calf of the same colour as herself, containing two beans and a barleycorn for each handful of curds. The man says to the woman:

"What dost thou drink?" To this she answers: "Generation of a male child." When the potion, the questions, and the responses have been repeated three times, the husband inserts in the wife's right nostril the juice of a fresh herb."[1]

Walking round the sacred fire is another rite said to induce conception. It is practised by the Brahmans of Dharwâr, while a priest recites a hymn.

The destruction of girls by the hands of their mothers is not sanctioned by religion; but public opinion and the law are not severe in regard to the practice. Many children of the female sex disappear; "they have been taken by wild animals." In 1870, three hundred girls from the town of Umritzar were carried away by wolves.[2]

[1] Quoted by Hartland from the "Sacred Books."

[2] E. S. Hartland, in "Primitive Paternity," writes:—"In the Panjâb, Hindu women who lose a female child during infancy, or while it still sucks milk, take it into the jungle and put it in a sitting position under a tree. Sugar is put into its mouth and a corded roll of cotton between its fingers. Then the mother says in Panjâbi—

> 'Eat the sugar; spin the cotton;
> Don't come back, but send a brother.'

If on the following day it be found that the dogs or jackals have dragged the body towards the mother's house, she considers it a bad omen, saying: 'Ah! she is coming back—that

"Let thy mother be to thee like unto a God." Notwithstanding, sorrow is the lot of the woman who is sterile, or who brings forth only girls. For her there is no adoration.

Child-marriage is another evil indicted by the Pundita Ramabai Sarasvati. This is one of the practices difficult to reconcile with the Hindu regard for the welfare of women. Dr. Coomaraswamy refers very briefly to the custom, and regrets that it still exists. I think I am right in saying that Miss Noble scarcely touches on the ethics of child-marriage in "The Web of Indian Life."

No choice in love is permitted to a Hindu maiden. Apologists for the marriage of arrangement explain that courtship begins after union, and that wooing usually ends with wedlock in the Western nations. This may be true in part; but the risk of incompatibility, or of sheer maladaptation, is very great when no selection whatever has been exercised by the contracting partners in conjugality.

In the case of a girl of nine years, taken as a wife, and kept by the bridegroom's mother until the nubile age, there is a chance of opportunities

means another girl.' But if it be dragged away from the home, she is glad, saying: 'The brother will come.' "

for learning something of a husband's character before the physical consummation. That is the only kind of courtship before wedlock.

In Bengal conjugal union with quite young children is still practised. Manu directs that girls of eight may be married, and that is the earliest age permissible. It is the usual custom to defer actual marriage until the bride has reached the period of puberty, which is usually supposed to occur at an earlier age in the East than in the West. There are, however, recorded cases of the marriage of girls under ten.

In 1890, fifty-five lady doctors petitioned the Viceroy and the Governor-General of India for an Act deferring the marriage of girls until the age of fourteen. Thirteen terrible instances of physical injury inflicted upon children, through premature union, were set down in the petition. In one case a child of seven died three days after the marriage ceremony.

In ancient times in India, it was decreed that husbands who cohabited with wives under ten years of age, with or without their consent, should be guilty of rape, and sentenced to life-long banishment, or imprisonment for ten years.[3] The age

[3] "A Practical View of the Age of Consent," Pamphlet, Calcutta, 1891.

of consummation was raised, some years ago, to twelve.

Mrs. Pechey Phipson, M.D., in an "Address to the Hindoos of Bombay on the Subject of Child-marriage," said that Indian girls are not physically adapted for maternity even when they have reached puberty. "A Hindoo girl of fifteen is about the equal of an English girl of eleven, instead of the reverse."

Premature marriage of girl-children is not restricted to India. It was practised in England in the time of Elizabeth; for an Act of her reign permitted legal wedlock with a child of ten. The marriageable age among the Esquimaux and other primitive peoples is frequently as early as in India.

The Pundita Sarasvati states that young wives are sometimes flogged by their husbands. This is, however, by no means a distinctly Eastern practice. Wife-beating is fairly common in almost every part of the world, and is practised with greater frequency in England than many persons imagine.

Medical science in India is in a backward state, although the treatment of disease is receiving more study, and modern methods are being introduced. The Pundita says that, through incapable treatment, a very large number of women die in India, and she attributes the high female mortality to this cause.

An instance of the conservative spirit of Hinduism has arisen lately (1913). The suffering woman of high caste runs the risk of grave religious and social censure if she undergoes an operation for the cure of a serious malady. Thus, the Maharanee of Indore had to come to England for an operation for appendicitis, and it is said that she incurred blame for breaking away from the tradition forbidding such relief.

This interdiction will probably disappear in the future. It affords an example of the apparently contradictory and inconsistent attitude of the Indian mind respecting the protection of women. A husband may not eat with his wife, nor see her taking a meal. She is encompassed by pious ceremony and ritual; and respect and even honour are accorded to her. But she must not be profaned by the touch of a man-surgeon, though her life is in peril. These anomalies in the treatment of Hindu women appear highly singular to Western people, who tend to outgrow their traditions more easily than the Orientals. Modern science, with its hostility to belief in fables, superstitions, and magic, is not in harmony with the credulous, imaginative Hindu outlook and veneration for old customs.

The position of widows is as unfortunate as that of childless women, or the mothers of girls. There are millions of widows in India, many of them young, and well constituted for remarriage and the functions of motherhood. Hinduism forbids the second union, though the law is being modified. A girl widowed at eighteen must remain celibate for the rest of her life. Judged from a racial hygienic standpoint alone, this restriction is injurious. The enforcement of widowhood for the whole of the puerperal life of a wife, whose husband has died while she was barely a woman, is, in both an individual and social sense, open to numerous objections.

Miss Noble might contend that the widow is perfectly resigned to her celibacy; that she is more than content in her loneliness. She is "a sacred mystery." Does this reflection console the mateless woman, left as a "child-widow" through the death of her betrothed?[4]

No doubt many widows in India are reconciled

[4] According to Dubois ("Hindu Manners") "the bare mention of a second marriage for a Hindu woman would be considered the greatest insult. She would be hunted out of society, and no decent person would venture at any time to have the slightest intercourse with her."

to their fate by the sainthood that the decease of a husband confers upon them. Maybe, numerous bereaved women experience pride in the honour shown to them by the traveller, who prostrates himself before them, and allows the dust of her feet to settle upon him as a benison. Our sympathy is not with these, but with the woman to whom love, a husband, and a family stand for all that is most desirable and precious in life.

Mrs. Krishnarao Bholanath Divatia, who contributes a section on "The Hindu Woman" to the volume "India," says that the condition of widows has been much misstated by foreign writers. She alludes to the happiness of Indian family life, and states that the widows are much honoured, especially if they are the mothers of sons. The remarriage of widows is now permitted by law in the Empire of India. It is not, however, popular, though it will no doubt become so. The same writer declares that polygamy is less fashionable than it was some years ago, and that educated men are opposed to the practice.

Her Highness the Maharani of Baroda pleads earnestly for the introduction of those British institutions to India that will be likely to benefit women. She gives a review of various employments which might be followed by her Hindu sisters. Her book "The Position of Women in Indian Life," has somewhat more of the spirit of the West than the East. Mr. S. M. Mitra, the well-known writer on Indian life, is very emphatic, in his introduction to the volume, concerning the need for reform.

"India must learn Western ways and keep pace with the West, or she must go to the wall. India must assimilate Western ways. Blind imitation will not do. The Indian must try to harmonize Eastern practice with Western civilisation."

An industrialised, commercialised India is apparently the ideal of the Western reformers. It is not the ideal of cultivated Hindu minds. We may admit that the East will profit by the example of the West in certain directions. But it is a lamentable fact that the implanting of Western virtues in Indian soil is accompanied by a crop of vices. "It is terrible to see how demoralizing our contact is to all sorts and conditions of men," says the author of "The Soul of a People."

On the other hand, the lady doctors of the Dufferin Association have rendered splendid service to Indian women and children. There is a very high rate of mortality among mothers and infants, due to careless treatment by native medical practitioners and midwives. Puerperal fever is common, and often proves fatal. The deaths in childbed are numerous.

"In Berar one-sixth, and in Bibar mainly one-fifth of the total number of females under ten are married."[5] The union is not very often consummated physically at this early age, but it is frequently consummated too soon for the well-being of the mother and her child. This marriage of immature girls is a drain on the vigour of the race, and is the cause of much suffering and illness. Procreative vigour declines somewhat quickly through misuse in adolescence. The menopause occurs earlier in Indian women than among the women of the West.

Hindu opinion concerning the disabilities under which women suffer in India is plainly expressed by a native writer Babu Nand Lal Ghose (Nandatela Ghosa) of Lahore.[6] This reformer has absorbed Western influence. While he professes the utmost admiration foı the many virtues of Hindu women, he deplores their limited lives, their conjugal inequality, and their defective education.

"Young India talks of political slavery, of foreign despotism, and of the British yoke, but these, if they really exist, are nothing in compari-

[5] "Imperial Gazetteer of India," 1908.

[6] "A Guide for Indian Females from Infancy to Old Age."

son with the despotism incarnate which rules the family life of the people, and until they reform that family life they will not be worthy to call for and to receive political freedom."

Nand Lal Ghose takes a Bengali woman as a type representing the indifferent social status of the Indian wife.

This writer gives a picture of the whole career of a Hindu woman from her birth in the zenana to old age. He asserts that children are brought into the world without adequate medical assistance. The midwives are chiefly of the low caste, and they are old women who know scarcely anything of maternity treatment. They occupy, however, an important position in India, and are called "second mothers." Many infants die through defective attention and a lack of knowledge of children's ailments.

The mother is convalescent for thirty-one days after the birth of her child. She then undergoes a ceremony, and is allowed to leave her couch. The suckling of infants is prolonged.

The Babu Ghose writes that Hindu girls are brought up strictly and practically secluded. Their diversions are few. They are fond of dolls, and they play at doll weddings. The Indian girl is capable of very warm friendships with girl companions. She goes to school, but the period of education is too short, as she usually marries before she is eighteen. At sixteen years of age, she is often already a mother. The girls of respectable families are not allowed to sing or dance, but sometimes they imitate the dancing of the nautch girls. Dancing is usually an art practised only by the professional dancers, who are not highly esteemed in society.

The system of marriage by parental arrangement is condemned by the Babu. He contrasts the custom with the freedom of selection permitted to Western women. Early marriage in India is attributable to the extreme dread of losing caste. It is most important that every well-born girl should be betrothed or married while still a child. This institution is of comparatively modern origin, and is contrary to the teaching of the "Sushrata," a famous medical work, which states that girls should not marry before sixteen, and that the husband should have reached the age of twenty-five. The protracted marriage ceremonies and rites are criticised by this writer. There is too much publicity and interference on the part of relatives. The bride and bridegroom know little or nothing of one another; yet they are united for life in the closest of human intimacies. The marriage of very young girls to adult men is strongly denounced by the Babu Nand Lal Ghose.

In an impartial spirit I have cited the views of both native defenders and critics of the status of women in India. No doubt the truth lies between the two points of view. But when educated and observant Englishwomen, reared in the traditions of Christian monogamy, assure us that Hindu women are happier wives than their sisters in England, and that family life is idyllic, we are bound to qualify the testimony of ardent Hindu critics. The strongest denunciations of social customs are often proclaimed by native reformers, and not by foreigners.

CHAPTER X

MOHAMMEDAN WOMEN IN INDIA

MOHAMMAD BARAKATULLAH, in her survey of Indian women under Moslem rule, writes:—

"To say that a Muslim harem is a pandemonium of misery, where women are caged like wild beasts, to toil and be tortured, is an assertion no less imaginary than a freak of fiction." [1]

This writer offers a tenable theory of Mohammed's sanction for isolation of women and polygamy. The Prophet found that, in Arabia, the sexes were living in considerable promiscuity and sexual disorder. He foresaw that the promulgation of a doctrine of strict monogamy would be sure to fail amongst a people so long habituated to licence, and he hoped that moral reform would follow the secluded life of women.

There is no precise encouragement of polygamy in the teaching of Islam. The Koran states that plurality of wives is permissible, under certain clearly defined and stringent regulations. A man must be sure, before marriage with more than one

[1] Vol. "India."

woman, that he will love one as well as the other; and this injunction is, in itself, of the nature of a deterrent. It means simply that a man must achieve a very powerful mastery over his natural preferences. Human nature being, as it is, such an impartial order of conjugal love, is not within the attainment of every man.

So strong is the insistence upon this absolutely equal distribution of a husband's affection, that men are warned of severe punishment in a future state of being, if they love one wife more than another. Recognising the risks of favouritism, Mohammed directs: "If you are afraid that you could not treat the wives with justice and equality, then marry only one."

Nothing could be plainer than this. And no doubt every devout Mohammedan strives to obey this imperative counsel. Probably, the monogamous Moslem is often swayed by this teaching. He fears that he may offend Allah by failing to love all his wives alike, and therefore he contents himself with one only.

Islamism is a comparatively new faith in India. Hinduism is not a propagandist religion. The creed of the Moslems is different; missionary zeal is one of the characteristics of the faithful. With the sword and suasion, and the use of the temporal powers, Mohammedanism spread over Persia, Turkestan, India, and into Malacca.

Some inquirers hold the view that Islam triumphed in India through a dissatisfaction with the caste system, and that converts were attracted by the more democratic temper of the alien religion. The question need not be discussed here. It is enough to say that the Indian Empire contains more followers of Islam than any other part of the globe.

The Moslem women of India hold a somewhat different position from that of the women of Arabia, North Africa, and Turkey. Unquestionably Mohammedan women enjoy numerous rights and privileges, though their sphere is limited practically to the home. But in family life, they are supreme. In some households, the wife exercises much higher authority than the husband, who hands over to her, not only the domestic sovereignty, but the conduct of important business affairs. If he wishes to sell property, he takes his wife's advice. Even in the matter of his dress, an Indian Moslem husband is under the direction of his spouse, and the most fashionably-attired men are those who rely upon their wives' taste.[2]

Christian missionaries in India have drawn dark

[2] "The Empire Series: India and Ceylon."

pictures of the "terrible degradation of Mohammedan women." The Rev. Joseph Cook, preaching in Boston, declared that there are 80,000,000 women in Moslem harems. "There are uncounted millions of men and women and children growing up in the most degrading superstitions, and suffering in mind, body and estate from inherited Pagan customs."

Sir Lepel Griffin stated some years ago that women in the past held, and still hold to-day in India "a great and often dominating influence in the domestic and political life of the country." Yet we are constantly assured by missionaries that Hindu and Mohammedan women are treated little better than animals.

The Rev. Dr. Elliott, of the Church Missionary Society, said, in an address[3] to the Zenana Missionary Society:—

"Mohammedanism is in its essence carnal, it is gross and sensual and it panders to the worst of passions, and it does not inculcate holiness. . . . It is a religion of grossness, sensuality, cruelty and darkness," etc.

Such extreme denunciation is far from uncommon in the literature of missionary organizations.

[3] "India's Women," Vol. XII., p. 436.

The following is a lady missionary's comparison of the Hindu and Mohammedan zenanas, written in 1892:—

Miss Harcourt, who has been one year at Bangalore, writes of it in the light of past experience in other parts of India.

"At first, in visiting the zenanas with Miss Smith, it was a great pleasure to me to note the good that was being done, and which was evident from the joy shown by the women in welcoming the ladies. Everything was full of interest, as I had never been among Mohammedans before. Their dress, manners, houses, are all very different from what I had seen in Tinnevelly amongst the Hindus and Brahmins. It struck me that these women are more affectionate, but—they have not the least idea of cleanliness!

"The children are dear, affectionate, little things, with bright black eyes; clothes of all colours cover their dirty little forms, they often wear red, blue, green, and purple together. But it does not look at all amiss on them, in fact, it is rather becoming to their dark skins. They are willing and anxious to learn, though not particularly bright, and they seem to look forward with very much interest to the daily half-hour Scripture lessons. The Word of God thus sown in the hearts of these children cannot be in vain." [4]

A proportion of missionary testimony must always be regarded with caution. Religious bias frequently tinges the statements to be found in the literature of all missions. This is inevitable. If we start with the postulate that an alien faith is "heathen," or "abominable," or "degrading," we

[4] "India's Women," Vol. XII.

are bound to exaggerate the evils, while we miss the benefits of the creed.

After reading missionary reports, one might reach the conclusion that Mohammedans are sheer barbarians, believing and practising a religion only adapted to low and ignorant savages. Such a view would be grotesque and grossly unfair. I have given the appreciations of orthodox Christian writers, free from that spirit of bigotry and rancour that so often distinguishes the ardent apostle of piety. These testimonies must be set by the side of the statements of crusaders, pledged to undermine the beliefs of a nation by all the methods within their power.

It is only common justice that we should consider both sides of this question dispassionately. The evidence of Syed Ameer Ali and Mohammed Baraktullah, two highly cultured Moslem writers, shows that the women of the Mohammedan religion in India are neither down-trodden, nor discontented. Indeed, they often enjoy a power and influence of great importance in society and in politics. Although the women of Bhopal are devout followers of Mohammed, their ascendency is so complete that they rule the state.

BURMESE LADIES AT A GARDEN PARTY

CHAPTER XI

MARRIAGE IN BURMA

ALMOST all of the writers upon Burma describe with enthusiasm the spell and the glamour of this beautiful country. We hear from visitors glowing reports of the happiness of the people, the delightful home life, and the attractive and amiable qualities of Burmese women.

Burma, with its flourishing capital Rangoon, is the largest province of India, and one of the most prosperous. The increasing population points to the comfort of the people and the vigour of the Indo-Chinese stock from which they descend. Quite ninety per cent of the natives are Buddhists. The system of education is better than that of most other parts of India, and, in the Western sense, the people are more progressive.

Polygamy is permitted in Burma; but the practice is not common, being confined almost entirely to a few upper-class families. Nevertheless, the tradition remains, and it has its influence upon the existing relations of the sexes. Though King Theebaw had only one wife, he lived in patriarchal grandeur, surrounded by a host of concubines and slaves.

There is no part of the East where marriage is as free as in Burma. Absolute sex-equality is said by some writers to exist here; and the liberty enjoyed by women so greatly exceeds all the privileges of their Hindu and Mohammedan sisters, that there is scarcely any comparison.

One of the most interesting phenomenon of the social life of Burma is the co-existence of a survival of mother-right and freedom for women in a community where polygamy is allowed and sometimes practised. Women not only dominate in the family, but they are entrusted with the most important business negotiations. In fact, the women of Burma are better merchants and traders than the men.[1]

Marriage among the Burmese is later than among the natives of most other parts of India, except in the region of the Parsees. In Burma girls do not marry till they are about seventeen, and from that age till twenty is the usual period for entering into wedlock. The offices of a priest are usually dispensed with by the couple, who undergo a simple ceremony, and eat rice together.[2]

The use of rice in marriage symbolism is com-

[1] "Among Pagodas and Fair Ladies," Gwendolen Trench Gascoigne.

[2] Gwendolen Trench Gascoigne, *Op. Cit.*

mon in many parts of the East. Rice, the staple diet of millions, is the most nourishing and plentiful of all the cereals, and it stands for an emblem of increase. Thus, the throwing of rice at bride and bridegroom in England is a survival of a ceremony of invocation to the gods to bless the pair with fertility. Confetti is now often substituted for rice in the towns, but the grain is still used in country districts of the United Kingdom.

There is no problem of celibacy amongst the Burmese. A man or a woman is considered quite incomplete until married. And as marriage is made very easy, and divorce no less facile, there is no reason why men and women should remain single. The abundant soil and the general prosperity of the country also favour marriage at an early age.

Divorce, though easily arranged, is as rare here as in other parts of the Indian Empire. Family life is usually very happy. There appears to be little marital incompatibility. Women are free within the home, and indeed, they usually rule in the domestic circle. Their influence in political and social affairs is not so palpable, but in business matters they often take the lead.

In a novel, entitled "A Marriage in Burmah," Mrs. M. Chan Toon gives an avowed faithful account of the life of an English girl married to a Burmese husband. As husband and wife were of different race, and held very dissimilar views, the novel cannot be taken as a fair presentment of ordinary monogamous marriage in Burma. The hero is depicted as selfish and intemperate. Towards the end of the story, he deplores that he has not had a son by a native woman, and he suggests to his English wife that she should select a Burmese girl to bear him an heir. The wife indignantly refuses, and announces that she wishes to have a son by a man of her own race. At this proposal, the husband is equally affronted.

Marriage between the Burmese, whether within or without the harem, rarely ends in the tragic fashion described by Mrs. Chan Toon in her novel. It would be difficult to point to any country where married life is as peaceful and idyllic as in Burma.

The women are usually slight and small in frame, and very graceful. Their eyes are dark and lustrous. In their long black hair they wear flowers. They love dancing and music, and are fond of festive gatherings in the open air.[3]

[3] Mr. Fielding, in "The Soul of a People," quotes these lines from a Burmese love-song:—"Her cheek is more beautiful than the dawn, her eyes are deeper than river pools; when she loosens her hair upon her shoulders, it is as night coming over the hills."

Everyone, including the children, smokes in Burma, and girls may be seen smoking big, strong cheroots, nearly a foot in length.

Regarding the constant use of tobacco, I may note here that some medical writers have asserted that smoking tends to induce sterility in both sexes. As the population of Burma is steadily increasing, in spite of incessant cigar-smoking by both men and women, to say nothing of young children, it seems necessary to examine more closely the evidence that tobacco produces infecundity; Professor Iwan Bloch asserts that it is not unusual in men addicted to smoking. It may be that the people of the Eastern countries resist the poison of nicotine more readily than those of the West. At any rate, the Oriental races that indulge in tobacco, and often immoderately, are by no means distinguished for a lack of virility and fecundity.

Coffee is also alleged to possess the same quality. Yet in Turkey, Egypt and among many Eastern peoples, strong black coffee is habitually consumed in large quantities.

The first sign of the change from childhood to adolescence in girls is made the occasion for a joyous ceremony. A family party is given by the parents, to which relatives and friends are invited. The girl is decked in her finest tamein, or robe, and she receives the congratulations of everyone present. A professional ear-borer is in attendance, who pierces a hole in the maiden's ears, so that she may wear from henceforth the large earrings that announce her attainment to womanhood.[4]

Boys in Burma, upon reaching puberty, undergo a ceremony of tattooing the legs with numbers of figures and artistic devices. There are various theories in explanation of the high position of women among the Burmese. Mr. Ferrass, who has given study to this question, remarks, in a letter to C. Gasquoine Hartley[5]:—

"There is evidence to show that at one time Burma was as densely populated as other fertile lands. A sort of War of the Roses prevailed there during the Sixteenth and Seventeeth Centuries, which reduced the male element enormously. The women had to take up all the agriculture and manufactures. They learned to become independent, and, having learned it, stuck to it. The character must have much to say to it, for there are African tribes in which the women are driven to do all the work, and are in consequence not more independent, but

[4] *Op. Cit.* by Miss Gascoigne.

[5] Mrs. Walter M. Gallichan, Author of "The Truth About Woman," "The Position of Woman in Primitive Society," etc.

less so than elsewhere. The Burman woman gives one the idea of being less feminine than the Chinese woman, on the one hand, and the Indian on the other. But which is here cause and which is effect? It is a very difficult problem. Certain it is that the women have now attained such a level of intelligence, and above all, of character, that they can hold their own in virtue of it. Whether they have those qualities by help of their opportunities, or the possession of the qualities made the opportunity, or both, it is hard, or impossible, to say."

"The Soul of a People," by H. Fielding, is a highly appreciative tribute to the fine qualities of the Burmese. There are three interesting chapters on "Women," in which the author's enthusiasm is infectious. The glow of the Burmese maidens' eyes is in these pages, and we get delightful glimpses of their home-life.

Mr. Fielding tells us that the women of Burma have the "hot love and daring of a man," and that they are "impulsive and full of passion." Sometimes they make the first advances in love. Passion is no mere passing incident in their lives. They live for love; it fills their whole emotion. At the same time, they all have work to do, and they are very rarely idle, like so many of the Mohammedan women. They perform men's labour in the fields and in carrying loads. Men in Burma sew and embroider. The women say that the men can do women's work better than a woman.

So hearty and wholesome is the love of life among these joyous optimists that it is difficult to persuade women to enter the religious houses. The Burmese girl does not wish to be a nun; she wants to taste all the pleasures of a healthy, normal life. She loves men, and wishes to bear children. Here is her sphere—in family love, the home, and domestic employments. The men are more inclined to pietism, and they often elect to live as monks. There are more monasteries than nunneries in the country.

Burmese women have the "rights" that they demand, and they have not been forced to fight for them. Buddhism has little or nothing to say for the position and the treatment of women. It is taken for granted that men are men, and women are women, and that the sexes want one another with an equal ardour. Sex equality comes simply and naturally among these cheerful, rational people.

There are very few divorces, for domestic concord is almost universal. Occasionally, there are tragedies, in spite of the prevailing felicity. Sometimes a girl commits suicide through unrequited affection, or through jealousy. Wheie love is accepted seriously we may expect to encounter the violent manifestations of passion.

Marriage is the destiny of every Burmese girl. But, as Mr. Fielding points out, the union of a pair of lovers is not a matter about which friends and neighbours are curious, as in the Western races. Burmese betrothed couples choose privacy rather than publicity, and weddings are very quiet affairs. There is no public show, such as we love in England. The bride and bridegroom enter into the civil contract, with but little ceremonial. Parade at such a time as this seems to them indecorous.

These fascinating people seem to me a race of artists. They esteem beauty, savour joy of life, and value love beyond riches. They hold revels and dances in the sunlight and open air. They toil industriously, but they play heartily and often. Have they not solved the secret of how to live?

The prosperity and the tranquillity of the Burmans are founded on sane social custom. I am inclined to attribute most of their well-being to the following excellent institutions and conventions:—

Freedom of selection, on the part of women, as well as men, in marriage.

The same standard of morality for both sexes.

Sharing of occupations and trades by men and women. There are very few idle women, as among the Western people, and in most parts of the East where polygamy prevails.

Fairly free social intercourse between the sexes.

Recognition of the supremacy of mothers in the home.

Facility of divorce.

Due estimation of the importance of the sex-passion as a social factor, and an absence of prudery.

The philosophic nature of the popular creed and its comparative latitudinarianism.

Rarity of harem isolation for women.

Early marriage with almost entire absence of celibacy.

No child marriage.

The high intelligence of women.

Legal equality for women.

CHAPTER XII

ZENANA MISSIONS

ABOUT the year 1807, William Carey, a native of Northampton, started a small society for the conversion of India to Christianity. He was assisted by the zealous Henry Martyn and two other clergymen. A few years later an English school was opened in Calcutta, in which Hindu children were instructed in the Bible.

Wilberforce approved of this mission, and lent it his fervent advocacy. Schools began to be erected in all parts of India, though the innovation was opposed by the natives.

"It is difficult to fix the exact date of the beginning of Zenana missions in Calcutta, as the necessity for them was felt simultaneously by all the Missionary Societies working in and around that city. Some say that the Baptist missionaries were the first to begin the work; and it is well known that Mrs. Mullens, of the L.M.S., and her daughters visited Zenanas in connection with their own mission at this time.

"In 1855 the Rev. J. Fordyce, who was then in charge of the Free Kirk Orphanage in Calcutta, employed one of his teachers, Miss Toogood, to visit in some Zenanas, to which access had been gained. She was followed by Miss Isabella Marr, who had been trained in the Calcutta Normal School, and the work soon fell into the hands of the Normal School

Society, and rapidly developed between the years 1859-1878. But in the early days of Zenana teaching there were great difficulties in the way. Prejudice was still strong, and often when a Zenana had been thrown open to the teaching of the missionary it suddenly closed again, causing great sorrow and disappointment to the teachers, who yearned for the souls of their poor imprisoned pupils." [1]

The movement grew steadily. A number of low-caste Hindus were attracted to the new creed, which offered them an ideal of democracy and fraternity, and promised a material heaven beyond the grave. There are now nearly three millions of Christian converts in India, mainly in Bengal and Madras.

The Church of England Zenana Missionary Society has stations all over the Indian Empire from Peshawar to Hyderabad, from Calcutta to Madras and Ceylon. There is no doubt that the lady medical missioners have done good work in the zenanas, where formerly the methods of healing were crude and inefficient.

There is, however, a difference of view amongst Anglo-Indians as to the ethical results of missionary enterprise. Certainly, only a few of the educated classes of India profess Christianity. The Mohammedans, who are becoming more numerous

[1] "India's Women," Vol. XII.

than the Hindus, are not readily persuaded to abandon their faith.

Mrs. A. M. L. Smith, a missionary, writing in 1892, asks: "What effect are we producing upon the Mohammedans of Bangalore? Humanly-speaking, we are so feeble—surrounded with difficulties, one and another often failing in health, the language strange to us, the people so far removed from our ways of thought that it is difficult for us to understand them—we cannot wonder that we cannot point to great results. But our faith is in God and we believe that His mighty Word will accomplish His Will even in our weak hands." [2]

Again, Miss Pontin, writing from Barrackpore, says: "One thought has been often in my mind during the past year; how very little we have yet done! how very little impression we have made." She continues that the Hindus are apathetic to the ministrations of the missionaries, and that there are few indications of a widespread conversion to the Christian religion.

Indian native publicists have, however, written commending the efforts of English missionary ladies, especially in the field of popular education and medical attention in the harems. The secular work of the Christian missions is in many respects

[2] Op. Cit., p. 409.

beneficial from the Hindu point of view. One native writer speaks with unqualified admiration of the Zenana Missions, describing them as "beneficent and ennobling agencies."[3]

It is fairly certain that the bulk of the Hindu and Mohammedan people of India will never embrace the Christian faith. The West has brought Christianity to the East; but the West has also introduced philosophic doubt and the rationalising tendency of the age. The message of the evangelical creed makes no appeal to the high-caste cultivated Hindu.

Any unprejudiced Englishman acquainted with Indian life will testify that we have made certain grievous mistakes in the administration of the Indian Empire. Tampering with ancient religious practice is always dangerous. The most sympathetic understanding and the rarest tact are necessary in dealing with the subject-races. These virtues are not always exhibited by administrators. "Our intolerance of a morality other than our own," writes Mr. J. H. Nelson, an English barrister, "brings about again and again the saddest results."[4]

[3] Babu Nanda Lal Ghose, "A Guide for Indian Females from Infancy to Old Age," Lahore.

[4] "The Scientific Study of the Hindu Law."

CHAPTER XIII

THE IMPERIAL HAREM IN TURKEY

THE plural system of marriage arose in Turkey among the mixed Caucassian races that came to be known as Turks. Descendants of a wandering Tartar horde, the founders of Turkey brought with them the customs of ancient Asia. Very early in their history they were polygamous; but to-day the Turks are said to be the least addicted to polygamy of any of the nations under the dominion of Islam.[1]

Ancient marriage in Turkey was a matter of negotiation and arrangement, and not of capture, as among the Arabs and some other Eastern tribes. To this day marriage is largely under the direction of a third person, or several persons, besides the contracting partners. The matrimonial agency is an old institution of the Ottoman Empire.

Although the great majority of Turks are married to one woman only, there are numerous harems in Constantinople and other towns. The sultans have always maintained plural marriage, and their harems have sheltered a large number of

[1] "Diary of a Turk," Halib Halid, 1903.

mistresses of all grades, besides the legal wives. A sovereign in Turkey is allowed to wed seven women. There is no restriction upon the number of his concubines and slaves; and some of the rulers have kept as many as a thousand women in their palaces.

Five thousand pounds a day has been stated as the cost of supporting a royal harem in Turkey. The pomp and grandeur of a sultan's court are beyond comparison. The ruler of the empire is a mighty autocrat to whom the utmost deference and obedience must be yielded. He must live in a truly regal state, befitting his exalted position.

For the sultans are not ordinary monarchs; they have despotic control of the souls and bodies of their subjects. They are the chiefs of the army, the supreme judges, and the kings. Behind the towering white walls of the Imperial Harem at Constantinople live thousands of persons of both sexes, all of them ministers and servitors to the pleasures of the Sultan. There is an army of eunuchs, and several hundred cooks, besides a multitude of slaves. The eunuchs who guard the approaches to the palace are all white men, who are not permitted to enter within. Negroes are the personal attendants upon the ladies of the court and the harem.

The Chief Master of the Maidens is a dignitary of unique eminence. He is almost feared by the Sultan himself. Here, as in Egypt, the *Kislar-aghasi* is like a king. His salary is enormous, and when he retires, he is entitled to a liberal pension for the rest of his days.

There are many well-paid officials in the royal household. The principal woman-supervisor controls a regiment of *Kalfas,* who have subordinates under their guidance. There are the "Mistress of the Sherbet," and the "Mistress of the Coffee," and numerous other female officials, all of them living in more or less splendour and authority. Their servants are the *alaiks,* who are practically slaves, though they have well-defined rights.

The Sultan's seraglio is adorned by the most beautiful women that Circassia can provide. Highest in rank is the mother of the heir to the throne, who possesses supreme privileges and a heavy dowry. The chief wives are next to her in station; and beneath them are the inferior wives, and the odalisques. Every woman in the palace is at the beck of the monarch.[2]

When a harem lady has been blessed by the admiration of her sovereign, she rises at once in posi-

[2] Several of my facts are gathered from Mrs. Bowman-Dodd's "Palaces of the Sultan."

tion. She is entitled to her own suite of rooms and attendants. A large sum of money is allotted to her, and she is secure and wealthy for life.

The slaves are selected for their youth and grace. In former days they were chosen in public, as in the Egyptian markets; but now the Sultan inspects the candidates in the harem, attended by the Chief Eunuch and other officers. These slave-girls are not treated with harshness, nor contempt. They have dainty fare, charming dresses, and comfortable chambers. If one shows an aptitude for music, the best instructors are provided for her training. Dancing is taught to all the girls, and many excel in the art, and become favourite performers. Care of the skin and the complexion and frequent bathing are enjoined.

A clever country maid may, by the exercise of her physical attractions, her wit, or her dancing, win the favour of the monarch. Many uneducated girls who enter the harem learn languages and become moderately well educated in a few months. A slave, if she is exceptionally intelligent, may become a teacher.

There is keen emulation among the host of slave-girls for the royal favour. Happy is the maiden who "has been looked upon." Her hour of triumph is near. An inquiring glance from her master's eye is the presage of good fortune, and she is set aside to await a summons to the royal chamber.

Many are the stories of crimes and cruelties perpetrated behind the forbidding walls of the harem. In bygone days, no doubt there were tragedies and horrors, though probably their frequency has been grossly exaggerated by foreign writers. I shall show presently that the Turk is not a truculent tyrant of women, and that the Turkish lust for cruelty has been overstated. Mohammed taught explicitly that servants should be treated with consideration and sympathy. The Prophet did not sanction slavery. Most probably the system was derived from the Hebrews. Turkish women of rank, who own slaves, are notably fair and kindly in their control of these attendants. Frequently the slave girl is a confidential companion, and a real affection exists between mistress and servitor.

At Garden Point, in Constantinople, the tourist is shown the spot where offending wives of the royal *serai,* or harem, were formerly cast into the Bosphorus, sewn up in a sack. "Thousands of women" are said to have received this capital punishment for adultery. Upon what authority are these accounts based? It is well-known that the affairs of the seraglio are conducted in the utmost secrecy. Who was present when hundreds of women were drowned at the same time? I do not say that such a penalty has never been inflicted upon erring wives; but I am disposed to ascribe much of this alleged cruelty to the imagination of prejudiced historians, hostile to the religion of Islam, and anxious to represent polygamy in its darkest aspects.

We have taken it for granted that the Sultan is the head and chief of the whole court and harem. To a large extent, this is true. But there is one who commands the sovereign, and is often feared by him. This potentate is a woman, the Validé Sultana, who reigns supreme over the great harem family. Here is highly instructive evidence of the persistence of the matriarchal authority in Turkey. The mother of the king is queen over the king and his family.

The Sultana-mother lives in magnificent apartments in the palace. Sixty of the handsomest eunuchs wait upon her, besides her female retinue. She supervises the women officials, and directs all the internal domestic affairs of the vast court. Her servants approach with folded arms, as a mark of humility and the highest respect. She is surrounded by the strictest ceremonial, and treated almost as a divinity. Every member of her family, from the Sultan himself, trembles at the thought

IN THE HAREM. TYPICAL COSTUMES OF CONSTANTINOPLE

of her displeasure. And yet we read of "the degraded position" of Turkish women. How can this be reconciled with the fact that the real autocrat of the royal harem is a woman?

If the Sultana Validé dies, the Sultan's wet-nurse is elevated to this royal position. A slave-girl may, through good fortune, become the Sultan-mother. Mahmud II. fell in love with a girl of the bath-chamber, and she bore Abdul Niedgid, who became ruler of Turkey. Thus the slave became Sultana Validé.

The life of the ruler of Turkey is not one of complete ease and luxury. As a prince, his probation is extremely austere. He is practically a prisoner, occupying the "cage," or *kafe,* for several years. In his own apartments, he is kept, uncontaminated by the outside world, under the direction of tutors and professors. It is true that he has several maidens and many servants to share his close seclusion. But his life is by no means idle and purposeless.

This training for the throne is succeeded by the responsibilities of government. The ruling of Turkey is not a sinecure. The position of Sultan becomes more and more difficult. Nominally, he is the supreme head of the dominion, but actually he is influenced by ministers and counsellors.

The very magnitude and opulence of the sovereign's possessions induce weariness and satiety. He strives to lead the simple life. Rising early, he performs his devotions, eats a plain, light meal, and receives his visitors. Those who seek an audience are received with courtesy and set at their ease. They are even permitted to sit by the Sultan on his divan.

Many of the Sultans may be described as having been domesticated. Almost all of them have proved good parents, and much attached to their children. Throwing aside the cares of the realm, they love to join the mothers and the children in the nursery, and to romp with the youngsters. The present Sultan is fond of horseback riding and sailing.

While a Jewess is never admitted to the Imperial *Serai,* there are several Christian women among the Sultan's train. They are well treated, and no intolerance is shown to their creed, which they are not asked to reject.

The daughters and sisters of the Sultan sometimes marry husbands without royal lineage. In these cases the husbands are extremely submissive to their wives; and they may not sit down in their presence without first asking permission.

The ladies of the Royal Harem wear costumes designed in Paris, and dress in the height of each changing fashion.[3] On State occasions of importance, they dress in the Turkish trousers and shawls. They are allowed to go out shopping in the bazaars, provided that they are suitably veiled.

The women of the seraglio often spend the day in boating, and they are fond of excursions into the country. Many parties of them, attended by their servants, go in carriages, and picnic in the woods. They play games and romp like children.

The Sultan has more than one palace, besides well-appointed houses for his favourite *ikbals.* These ladies live apart from the *serai,* and have their own guards and servants. They entertain their royal spouse in their own residences.[4]

The slaves of the royal household fare as well as the ladies whom they attend; and their lot is certainly easier than that of most servants in Christian countries. Mrs. Garnett thinks that, in many respects, the Turkish female slave is better off than the domestic servant of the West. At the end of

[3] Lady Duff-Gordon, writing to "The London Budget," Nov. 23, 1913, says that in Paris "the harem influence continues to be strongly evident in the fashions of the winter. . . . The harem dress is the dress of allurement. No Occidental woman understands the mystery, the depth of allurement, as Oriental women do."

[4] See Mrs. Lucy M. J. Garnett's interesting volume, "Women of Turkey." II. *Ibid.*

seven years of servitude, she is a free woman, and often a husband and a dowry are found for her. If she is beautiful and amiable, she may rise to a very enviable position in the *serai*.

CHAPTER XIV

POLYGAMY IN TURKISH SOCIETY

A TURKISH gentleman informs me that the *serai* may, in the near course of time, become quite rare and curious in his country. Monogamy is now considered "good form," and plural marriage is beginning to be regarded as old-fashioned. Turkey has always been very susceptible to alien influences. She has during later years absorbed much of the spirit of the West; and Turks who have lived for some time in England or France, return to their land with a new perspective of social life and ideals.

The bulk of the population of Turkey is monogamous. It would be correct to state that the polygamists are an almost insignificant number, confined entirely to the rich class. Many men married to one wife keep mistresses in a second establishment; but the lords of the large harems are few.

The ownership of a *serai* imposes several severe obligations apart from the high cost. A Turk cannot follow the example of the West, where the "kept woman" can be repudiated and cast aside, even if she is penniless. The law and public opinion of Turkey demand that a husband or a lover must provide for the discarded wife, or mistress, as well as the children of the union.

A prudent Turk, before venturing upon plural marriage, reflects that the claims of his wives and concubines are numerous and heavy. Custom is exacting in this matter. Several wives require several servants, separate apartments, carriages—for harem women do not walk out of the harem grounds—expensive fashionable gowns and hats, jewellery, and, above all, generous dowries. Eunuchs must be kept and well paid, for they are indispensable. There are a hundred-and-one incidental expenses to be reckoned with. Moreover, several wives mean a big family. And in Turkey, where family affection is deep, a father is bound by conscience and the law, to maintain his offspring in comfort, and to provide for their future.

Besides the economic deterrent, there is the growing sentiment against polygamous unions. A cultured Turk, with a cosmopolitan experience, ponders upon the family life of the monogamous countries, and discovers something admirable in its loving comradeship with one woman. He deplores the defective education of the mass of women in his own country, and asks whether polygamy is not in a large degree the cause of this.

In many respects single marriage in Turkey affords a sound example to England and America. Divorce, though simple, is very rare. In the Western societies, where it is difficult, it is quite common. I think the scarcity of separation may be accepted as a tribute to the conjugal adaptability of the Turks. They make good husbands and wives. From all that I know of the men of Turkey, I am convinced that they excel in that sympathetic understanding of women which generally ensures success as a lover and husband.

Let us consider for a moment the temperament and character of the Turks. They are not so completely "Oriental" as the Hindus. The race is very mixed, and there is a strong strain of Circassian blood in the highest families. The salient traits of the Turk are ardour in sexual love, quick temper, fortitude, kindliness, and courtesy. Social intercourse is democratic; there is not a wide gulf of caste between employer and employed, and between master and slave.

A conspicuous quality of the Turk is his devotion to family life and his great affection for children. He not only loves his own children, but his tenderness extends to all children. Perhaps nowhere else can such fond fathers be found in the East or West.

Thackeray was impressed by the love of the

Turkish people for their children. "I never saw more kindness to children than among all classes, more fathers walking about with little solemn Mahometans in red caps and big trousers, more business going on than in the toy-quarter, and in the Atmeidan." And he gives a description of grey-beards finding the greatest delight in playing with young children.

This love of children is confirmed by Sir Edwin Pears, in "Turkey and its People." "Paradise is beneath the ground over which mothers walk," said Mohammed. This esteem for maternity and gentle solicitude for the well-being of the young is one of the most beautiful traits of the Turkish character.

The man who understands children, and is loved by them, has certain qualities that appeal to women. Women say that tenderness is one of the virtues that they most esteem in men. This tenderness is nearly always apparent in the Turk. He is a born wooer, possessed of sympathetic insight into woman's inner soul. Art develops this natural gift; for the men of the East are diligent students of the art of love. Compared with them, the average Briton is an inexperienced amateur.

Regarded from the question of ensuring happy and healthy marital relations, Sir James Paget has some wise words upon our disastrous ignorance of the physical expression of conjugal love. No Oriental is allowed to marry in such ignorance. Turkish and Persian love poetry reveal this masculine appreciation of woman's nature. There is no doubt that the tranquil, felicitous married life in Turkey is due largely to the pains that men take in learning the art of love.

There is no rending sex-antagonism in Turkey, as in England at the present day. Men and women accept one another joyfully as gifts from the gods. They fulfil their sex-lives naturally, without concern as to which sex is the more virtuous or superior. I am not assuming that all is wrong with our own marriage system and that everything is right with wedlock in Turkey.

There are, however, certain sane and beneficial customs in Turkey that other nations might imitate. English and American women, who have seen the inner home-life of the Turks, frequently assert that the women are, on the whole, in a better position than in any other country of Europe; indeed, one American lady has declared that women in Turkey are more esteemed, and have higher privileges, than in the United States.[1]

[1] See "Palaces of the Sultan," Anna Bowman Dodd, and Mrs. Garnett's "Women of Turkey."

Lady Mary Wortley Montagu gives several pictures of Turkish harem life in her time. At Adrianople, she paid a visit to a *serai* containing about two hundred women. She was received with the utmost courtesy.

> "The first sofas were covered with cushions and rich carpets, on which sat the ladies, and on the second their slaves, behind them, but without any distinction of rank by their dress, all being in a state of nature, that is, in plain English, stark naked, without any beauty or defect concealed. Yet there was not the least wanton smile or immodest gesture among them. They walked or moved with the same majestic grace, which Milton describes our general mother with. There are many among them as exactly proportionate as ever any goddess was drawn by the pencil of Guido or Titian, and most of their skin shiningly white, only adorned by their beautiful hair, divided into many tresses, hanging on their shoulders, braided, either with pearl or ribbon, perfectly representing the figures of the graces."

Mohammedan modesty is chiefly manifested by women in the practice of covering the face from the gaze of the other sex. There is much less solicitude for concealing the body. Friends who have surprised Eastern women, when bathing in the rivers, tell me that the women run to put on their veils, and so long as their faces are covered, they are not concerned about the rest of their figures. But we are told that Mohammedan women are shocked at the evening dress of English women.

The Turkish veil is a more complete covering for the face than the Arab *yashmak.* It is of muslin, and covers the whole head. Over the veil is worn a hood, attached to an unlovely garment that reaches to the heels and encases the body.

In the East there is a reluctance on the part of well-bred women to show the feet. Turks are inclined to make a fetich of their women's feet, somewhat after the manner of the Chinese. Strabo refers to "the courtesan Rhodope, whose sandal was carried off by an eagle and dropped in the King of Egypt's lap as he was administering justice, so that he could not rest until he had discovered to whom this delicately small sandal belonged, and finally made her his queen." [2]

A Turkish beauty's slippers are an important part of her clothing. The foot has an erotic significance among most Moslem peoples, and, to a certain extent, in Spain, which owes many of its ideas and practices to the Moorish conquerors. Students of sexual psychology are aware that boot-and-shoe fetichism is common in most countries.

The same passion for powerful scents that pre-

[2] Quoted by Havelock Ellis, "Erotic Symbolism," "Studies in the Psychology of Sex," Vol. V.

vails amongst the Egyptian women is noted in the harems of Constantinople. There is very frequent reference in Oriental love poems to the odour of the loved one. Odorous tresses are described, and likened to the smell of musk and civet. This keen olfactory sensitiveness is normal in Arabia and Turkey. The Turks love the heavy perfume of the lily. They are especially fond of musk and myrrh, and women often use strong perfumes in their baths and unguents. The "lotus woman" of the Hindus, the flower of her sex, should possess the natural aroma of musk. In the "Song of Songs," which is typically Oriental, we read of "myrrh," "spices," and "sweet herbs."

The *haremlik,* or the women's quarters, in the houses of Turkish aristocrats is furnished in modern European style, the fittings and furniture tending to lose their Eastern character. English pianos are to be seen.

The ladies of the *haremlik* can gaze upon the outer world through apertures in the darkened windows, but they are not seen from without. They go out at will, like the women of the Imperial Harem, but always veiled.

Dancing is one of the accomplishments of the women of the seraglio. The Turkish dancers sway the upper part of the body from the hips, and often writhe with snake-like motions. The feet play a subordinate part in most Oriental dances; but the arms are in constant waving motion, sometimes extended on either side, or raised above the head.

Among the troupe of Turkish dancers who appeared in London a few years ago, many of the performers were very proficient in a peculiar movement of the head from side to side without any motion of the neck. This is an important feature of dancing in Turkey, and the movement is strangely suggestive of dislocation of the neck. It appears to be extremely difficult, but a Spanish professional dancer, with whom I am acquainted, tells me that she learned the head movement in about a week by practising in front of a mirror.

The dances are often protracted, and very exhausting to the artists. Whirling round at a great rate is a part of the art. This giddy evolution is sustained for many minutes, and causes a sense of vertigo in the spectator. The girl becomes almost frenzied. She whirls faster and faster, and finally reels to a couch, her face drenched and white, almost in a state of collapse from the prolonged and violent exertion. Most of the dancers are voluptuous, and describe amorous passion. They are less graceful and pleasing than the peasant dances of Spain.

Although some Turkish women are excellent dancers, they are not fond of physical exercise, and the sporting or athletic woman is unknown in the society of Constantinople. The men are often fine equestrians, and some are formidable wrestlers, but they have no liking for field-sports.

Devotions, the toilet and bathing occupy much of the women's time. They are very fond of the hot vapour bath and the heated chambers, and some of them will spend the greater part of the day at the *hammam*.

No harem *ikbal* allows her hair to turn grey. Such sign of age must be remedied by every device of art. Dye is used constantly for the hair upon the first appearance of fading. Wrinkles in the skin of the face are treated by massage and emollients.

Although the Turks excel in affection for their children, infant mortality is high owing to defective hygiene and the incompetence of physicians. The secluded life of the women in the seraglio, and the average home in Turkey, is not the best environment for mothers. It cramps the intelligence, and perpetuates antiquated and often foolish and injurious practices in the rearing of infants. The nurses in the harem are not properly trained, and many children die through their mismanagement.

Women of the *haremlik* have the chief care of their children during the years up to the marriageable age, and their influence is great during childhood and adolescence. Being imperfectly educated, and inexperienced in all that concerns the larger life of the world, the average Turkish mother, in spite of her parental tenderness, is not often a competent instructress of the young. She is almost always very conservative in her views and her habits, and she accepts all the ideals in which she has been trained from earliest infancy. The spirit of "the unchanging East" fetters and cramps her mind.

Upon this influence of the mothers Halib Halid has some reflections in his interesting "Diary of a Turk," published in 1903.

The mixture of the white and the more pigmented races in Turkey has produced a distinct type of beauty amongst the women. Many Turkish ladies are fair, with grey or blue eyes and light brown hair. Some are handsome brunettes, with luxuriant black hair. The eyebrows are rather heavy and arched.

A Turkish beauty has tender, almond-shaped eyes, with pointed corners to the lids. Her face is often "made up" with various powders and rouge, and the rim of the eyelid is stained. In form the women of Turkey incline to plumpness and roundness, but they are often finely modelled. Their attractions begin to fade before middle-age, in spite of bathing, massage, and constant attention to the preservation of their good looks and their figures.

About a century ago, Lady Craven wrote:—"I think I never saw a country where women may enjoy as much liberty and fear from all reproach as in Turkey." This opinion is confirmed by almost all the observant travellers whom I have questioned, and in numerous volumes to which I have referred. Several English women have written of the women of Turkey as down-trodden, immured and secluded, but such a view is scarcely just. Certainly, judged from a purely Western standpoint, Turkish women are debarred from specific forms of freedom enjoyed in Christian countries. But when a balance is struck, we shall perhaps realise that the difference between the status of the English woman and her sister in Turkey is not so marked as it appears.

Turkey has solved the problem of involuntary celibacy for women, which is one of the most palpable defects of the monogamous marriage system. We have tens of thousands of spinsters who are actually doomed to the single life against their inclination, to say nothing of a large number of women who profess a preference for celibacy. Such a phenomenon is quite incomprehensible to the Eastern intelligence. The main function of woman, from Nature's decree, is reproduction, and this the Oriental accepts without hesitation. Infecundity is the worst misfortune that can befall a Turkish or Hindu wife. More wretched still is the state of celibacy, except when voluntarily adopted, as in the case of priestesses and saints.

Enforced continence for numbers of women, and prostitution, the twin evils inseparable from monogamy, are mitigated, if not entirely banished, in polygamous states. Lifelong virginity is practically unknown in the East. The social evil exists, but to a limited extent, and under different conditions from those prevailing in Christian monogamic societies.

"Sacred prostitution" was in reality a rite for the promotion of fertility. The paramours of the women in the Temple of Mylitta repeated the words, "May the goddess be auspicious to thee!" showing clearly that the ritual had a fecundating meaning. The forms of prostitution surviving in the East are plainly derived from old religious observance, and originally they were not of a mercenary or vulgar character, but of very sacred and serious import.

Among the Corinthians this practice began to lose its pious associations. The priestesses were ministers to men rather than to the deity. This transition is explained by Havelock Ellis in his valuable examination of hetairism[3] from the earliest ages. Whenever Mohammedans and Hindus have come into relation with Western conquerors, traders, and travellers, prostitution has arisen and spread. In Burma the custom was unknown before the advent of the English. And so with the whole of India.

Mohammed denounced prostitution, and it was scarcely known in Moslem countries during the first centuries of the faith. Nowadays, the evil is fostered by the constant influx of foreigners in the Eastern cities. For example, in Turkey, the keepers of brothels are usually Jews, and their chief patrons are Christians. The same may be said for Egypt. Sir Edwin Pears, in "Turkey and Its People," 1911, writes that the social evil is apparent in Constantinople. On the other hand, I have been informed by friends who have lived in Turkey that there is comparatively little prostitution.

Mrs. Anna Bowman Dodd and Mrs. Lucy M. J. Garnett, to whose writings I have referred, pre-

[3] *Op. cit.*

sent the views of cultured observers upon the status of the women of Turkey. Neither of these ladies have dwelt only on the darker aspect of the lives of Mohammedan women and the "degradation" of the *haremlik.* Their testimony is impartial, and therefore valuable.

CHAPTER XV

FEMINISM IN TURKEY

THE title of this chapter will seem a misnomer to those who hold the preconceived view that Mohammedan women are hopelessly crushed beneath male tyranny, and devoid of most of the common rights of human beings. It is not unusual to hear critics in the West assert that "no women under Islam can enter Paradise," and that Mohammed insisted upon the inferiority of the female sex to the extent of likening them to mere animals, "asses," and the like.

There are passages in the Koran bearing upon the proper conduct of women, which inculcate humility and modesty. Precisely similar teaching may be found in the epistles of St. Paul, the supreme Apostle of ecclesiastic Christianity. Women were bidden to learn of men, to stay at home, not to speak in the public assemblies, to avoid vanity, to dress plainly, and to obey their husbands in all things.

St. Paul's view of marriage was that of the ascetic saints who succeeded him. He had no fine, spiritual appreciation of love and the married

TURKISH BRIDE IN WEDDING DRESS

state. Marriage was a method of avoiding carnal sin.

The Prophet of Mecca proclaimed a nobler estimate of wedlock, though this will be disputed by the extremists who cannot separate polygamy from innate iniquity in those who practise it. Liberal orthodox Christians have, however, admitted justly that a man with more than one wife is not of necessity an immoral character. They recognise that some of the most righteous of mankind have been supporters of polygamous marriage. The following passages from the Koran, while they enjoin modesty and restraint upon women, are less patriarchal in spirit than the injunctions of St. Paul:—

> "And speak unto the believing women, that they restrain their eyes, and preserve their modesty, and discover not their ornaments, except what necessarily appeareth thereof; and let them throw their veils over their bosoms, and not show their ornaments, unless to their husbands, or their fathers, their husband's fathers, or their sons, or their husband's sons, or their brothers, or their brothers' sons, or their sisters' sons, or their women, or the captives which their right hands shall possess, or unto such men as attend them and have no need of women, or unto children, who distinguish not the nakedness of women.
>
> And let them not make a noise with their feet that their ornaments which they hide may thereby be discovered."

Making a noise with the feet refers to the tinkling ornaments and bells that the women of the Prophet's time wore upon their ankles.

If the women of Turkey have not attained to those forms of freedom in society enjoyed by English and American women, they have a much firmer security in a legal sense. There was no need for a Married Woman's Property Act in the Ottoman Empire. Complete possession and control of the personal property of women was granted ages ago.

Every Turkish mother has sole guardianship of her children in their early years. In after life, the children seek her counsels, and the sons frequently obey their mothers during the whole of their lives. Upon divorce or repudiation by a husband, all of a wife's property is allotted to her.

It is supposed that divorce is impossible for a woman in Turkey. This is incorrect. There are several causes for a legal separation from a husband. Cruelty, and even neglect to maintain a wife in the station in which she was born, are reasons for a woman's plea for divorce. Desertion by a husband is another cause. If a wife wishes to leave a husband on any of these charges, she is entitled by law to a return of the dowry paid upon marriage.

"Turkish women," writes Mrs. Garnett, "thus already possess all the legal personal and proprietary rights necessary to give them a social position equal, if not superior, to that of European women generally; and the objection to their emancipation from harem restraints is consequently one of custom and prejudice rather than of religious law, the seclusion of women and the veiling of the face being immemorial social usages borrowed from other neighbouring Oriental races, and not institutions peculiarly Turkish, and no religious law would, therefore, be contravened by a change in these merely social customs."

Returning once more to the question of divorce, we must realise that it is not quite as simple a matter as it appears. A devout Mohammedan shrinks from casting aside his wife, unless the reason for so doing is exceptionally definite. He remembers the stern words of the Prophet: "The curse of Allah rests on him who capriciously repudiates his wife."

Critics of Islam, who state that the men of the East "treat women as chattels" while they are of use—and discard them with sheer callousness when they have lost the freshness of youth—should consider the testimony of the many Christian observers of Turkish home-life. As a matter of fact, in many harems old women will be seen leading contented and happy lives, surrounded by relatives and young children. The Turk does not turn out his grandmother to starve in the streets. He has rarely any inclination to do so. Moreover, his creed and the law do not allow it.

In a spirit of fair inquiry, we must listen to those travellers in Turkey who do not share the optimistic view of the writers I have quoted, and the friends with whom I have conversed. There are still Occidental visitors who speak of unfortunate women in Turkey, pent up in the harems, and living degraded lives as the mere instruments of sensual men.

Sir Edwin Pears, in the work to which I have referred, is not so prejudiced an investigator as some of my compatriots. He admits that there are admirable traits in the Turkish people, and he testifies to their love of children. But this author's impressions are very different from those of Mrs. Garnett, who lived so long in Turkey, and has studied the inhabitants of town and country with much zeal and intelligence.

Sir Edwin Pears finds an absence of family life, whereas other strangers in the land seem to discern domestic affection and tender conjugal love in almost every home.

In the East husbands and wives do not walk arm-in-arm in the streets. Frequently, as in India, the man walks in advance of the woman. This is, however, no sign of an open assertion of male superiority. It has a very different origin. In the old times, the husband strode in front of the wife, to hold back the branches of the forest and to make a track for her. He was like a military vanguard, ready for encounters with enemies, and not the leader of a weak and submissive spouse, who was not worthy to walk at his side.

Sir Edwin Pears declares that the hold of a wife upon her partner is exceedingly insecure. In a fit of temper, or in a moment of caprice, the husband may say: "I repudiate you." But repudiation is not easy, and, according to other witnesses, it is not frequent. Nevertheless, the custom exists, and its existence is deplored by many thoughtful and high-principled men in Turkey.

"Whatever the recent teachers of Islam may say," writes Sir Edwin, "it is, however, beyond reasonable doubt that the position of women in Moslem is lower than in Christian countries."

I have already given distinctly contrary opinions expressed by English and American women. It would be absurd to pretend that cultured women in Turkey have all that they desire, intellectually and in the social sense. There is even a franchise movement among the educated women. Certainly, no country has yet been discovered in which there is no need of reforms; and it is true of Turkey to-day that discontent among upper class women is not altogether uncommon. I believe that this spirit of dissatisfaction is not always associated with the institution of polygamy. It is a desire for freer social intercourse, for culture, and for a widening of women's interests and pursuits.

The students who attend the women's college at Scutari are likely to develop into ardent pioneers of a feminist movement in Turkey. Among our Suffragist leaders are a quite imposing number of women who are distinguished as scholars. Education in any and every class gives rise inevitably to "divine discontent." Very frequently the widening of knowledge brings an awakening of conscience and a quickening of the social instinct. Women who learn to think begin to feel more deeply; and reflection upon the evils of society leads to action.

The national temper in Turkey is conservative; but, as I have said, the Turk is always a willing listener to the ideas and the reformative proposals of foreigners. Despite tenacious traditions, the women of Turkey are feeling the influence of that fervent feminism that is inspiring the women of the West. There is, perhaps, more hope for Turkish women in this movement than for any of the women of Europe. And a reason for thinking so is based upon the modesty and reasonableness of their demands and the method pursued. Already men in Turkey are attentive to the arguments of cultivated women, and there is, as yet, no apparent masculine opposition.

The Young Turkey Party, in the opinion of Mrs. Garnett, advocates the emancipation of women. The Turk is pre-occupied with women, but this pre-occupation does not spell only one kind of interest. The great feminists among men are the great lovers of women, the admirers of womanly beauty, grace and wit.

We have noted that the *haremlik* has reached a stage of something like unpopularity. Polygamy is not likely to give place rapidly to universal monogamy in Turkey. We might as well expect to banish polygyny suddenly from Western societies. But the stricter rule of the seraglio is relaxing. Even doctors are allowed to enter the harems. Culture is invading the sacred precincts of "the Abode of Bliss," and culture brings a longing for a freer life. The West of Europe is setting Turkey an example, for good or ill, and Turkey is at least heedful and interested. The ground is being sown. What will the future yield?

Is East eternally East? Turkey, at all events, is the most sensitive of all Eastern nations to the influence of outside social movements. In certain respects she admires England, and is willing to imitate English customs. Not even the influence of Mohammedism can withstand the irresistible force of human thought and social progress. Probably much that is admirable in Turkish custom will decline with the incoming of Western industrial and commercial ideals. Possibly there will be social gain also. Who can foretell? That which we laud as progress in the West is not always a boon to the East.

Are we happier in our pseudo-monogamic, jostling, commercial, spiritually-deadening civilisation? The answer is doubtful to all but the unreflective.

Pierre Loti, who feels, like a true artist, the strange enchantment of the Orient, has interested himself very closely in the affairs of Turkey. He has many friends in the country, and his penetrating mind discerns all the signs and symptoms of impending changes in the position of Turkish women.

Loti's novel "Disenchanted" reveals the soul of a woman in the *haremlik*. He tells us in his preface that the volume is one of fiction. But the author insists that it is entirely true, in so far as it demonstrates the advance in culture among the women of Turkey secluded in the seraglios. This spread of knowledge is yielding the inevitable dissatisfaction that the repressed sex naturally experience when they begin to reflect. The Woman Movement and Labour Unrest spring everywhere from education.

Sober-minded and thoughtful Turks are beginning to ponder on the Woman Question. They foresee that educated women will rebel sooner or later against many of the old traditions of religion and society. The spirit of England and France is permeating the harems. Women dress in the English and French fashions; they demand English furniture and pianos. They are learning foreign languages, and reading the literature of the West. Some of the Turkish ladies eagerly imbibe the new social ideas.

Pierre Loti's romance is not merely a pathetic story. It is a contribution to the sociology of the Near East. The heroine voices the aspirations of the new woman of Turkey. She cries out for light, for liberty in the supreme matter of choice in love, and for contact with the great world outside of the seraglio. The novel describes faithfully the narrow environment in which harem women live. Loti shows how the disenchanted yearn for love. The heroine of the story says:—

"She has achieved the sort of duality of identity which is common to many Turkish women of her age and rank, who say: 'My person is delivered over by contract to an unknown man, and I devote it to him because I am an honest woman; but my soul, which was not consulted, is still my own, and I keep it with jealous reserve for an ideal lover whom I may never meet with, and who in any case will never know anything about it.'"

The heroine of Loti's romance refers to the loneliness of seraglio life:—

"The sense of emptiness which is produced in our life by the necessity of never talking to any but women, of living always among ourselves, our fellow-women. Our friends? but, mercy; they are as weak and as weary as we are! In our harems weakness—so many weaknesses rather, combined and huddled together, are sick at heart, suffer the more from being what they are, and cry out for strength."

CHAPTER XVI

THE HAREM IN MODERN EGYPT

THE significance of the word harem has been interpreted variously as "that which is forbidden" and the "Abode of Bliss." These establishments, in which women are segregated in luxurious surroundings, exist in much of their former splendour in Cairo to-day.

The round, central hall, roofed with a high dome, is in some harems about one hundred and fifty feet across. Around this spacious apartment are divans of red velvet. In the centre there is, in some instances, a sunk circular bath.

The following description of the interior of a regal harem in Egypt is taken chiefly from Miss Lott's "Harem Life in Turkey and Egypt."

The whole of the floor is covered with a thick, handmade carpet, very soft to the tread. Women and eunuchs pass to and fro noiselessly.

Innumerable doors, each one a mirror, surround the interior of the great hall. These are the entries to the apartments of the women. In all these chambers is a connecting door through which the pasha can pass at will. The walls are very beautifully decorated with painted panels of birds and flowers in gorgeous colours. In many harems the bath is in one of the arms or wings, or in a separate building in the gardens. A solid stone wall, thirty feet in height, encompasses the palace and the delightful gardens.

The chief apartments of a Grand Pasha's daughters in Cairo have been described by Emmeline Lott, in her book on "Harem Life," as two large saloons. The carpets are of the finest Brussels. On the carpets are innumerable spots of melted wax that have fallen from the candles carried in the fingers of the slaves. Divans, covered with fine red damask satin, surround the room.

A tall mirror reaches from the floor to the ceiling. In one corner of the mirror fruit and flowers are painted; in others, musical instruments, weapons, and the crescent. The marble tables are supported on gilt legs, and upon each table is a silver chandelier holding eight candles. The candles have red glass shades, adorned with paintings of flowers.

Seven rooms, approached from the saloons, are used as bedchambers. One of these rooms had a divan covered with striped red and green damask, standing near a window overlooking the pasha's garden. Damask hangings were attached to the window and the door. No blankets are used, but a wadded coverlet was spread on the bed. Landscapes were painted on the ceiling, from which was suspended a huge gilded chandelier. On the walls were designs of flowers.

In the lovely scented gardens were myrtle hedges enclosing borders of luxuriant roses. Jessamine, with white and yellow blossoms three times the size of these flowers in England, trailed everywhere. Dazzling geraniums carpeted some of the beds. The air was odorous with the leaves of the verbena tree and the rose. Oranges and many other fruits abound. Huge cacti and strange Indian plants flourish here.

The square sheets of ornamental water have each their pagoda of white marble. Within these are comfortable divans. Around the lakes are terraces of marble, with vases decked with sweet-smelling flowers. China cushions, exquisitely painted to resemble silk, are placed at the corners of the terraces. Upon the gates of the garden are life-size marble figures of lions. In the gardens are statues of nude men and women.

Marble lions adorn the terrace steps leading to the pleasure boats. Swans, black and white, swim in the clear water. Numerous aquatic birds of the most beautiful plumage frequent the lakes. On the roof of the pagoda Egyptian crows, with sheeny black wings, build their nests.

There are mazes in these fairy gardens formed of myrtle hedges. Near the mazes are huge marble fountains, the basins supported by female figures from whose mouths sparkling water spurts. In the centre of one fountain is an immense statue, in marble, of Ceres, carrying on her hand a basket of fruit and flowers, coloured in imitation of nature. The goddess holds in her hand a cornucopia filled with ears of wheat and bunches of black and white grapes.

Around the fountains are terraces of marble upon which stand light ironwork tables and couches. The fountains are surrounded and shaded by weeping willows, and among the trees are numerous statues.

Every garden has its swings for the women. Swinging is a favourite Oriental pastime, and in some of the temples of India swings are provided for both men and women. In the paintings of the school of Watteau, women are frequently represented in swings, surrounded by admiring gallants.

The swings of the harem gardens are shaped like barouches, and recall the swing-boats of our

English fairs. They are fitted with cushions. From the garden one passes into a superb hall floored with marble, and with a ceiling gleaming with gold, supported by twenty-eight to thirty pink marble columns with carved capitals.

In another sumptuous harem, the halls are of marble, surrounded by a verandah, with many columns of porphyry. Vases, with rams' heads, and horns as handles, stand on the terraces, and are filled with choice semi-tropical plants. At night the verandah is illuminated by gilt lamps. The gorgeous rooms of this palace are carpeted with a material resembling the softest green mosses of several shades. All the ceilings in the larger chambers are painted with designs and figures of men, women, and animals, or scenes in Cairo and Alexandria, Cleopatra's Needle, and parts of the banks of the Nile. Four immense stained glass windows shed a tinted light in the hall. The hangings of the doors and windows are of white satin, upon which flowers are printed.

There are no divans here, but chairs, sofas, and footstools of ormolu and gold. Almost the whole of the wall space is occupied by high glittering mirrors, giving the effect of a huge glass curtain. The clock on the mantelpiece is of modern manufacture, much gilded. Two massive candelabras are on either side, each holding twelve wax candles.

A drawing-room adjoining is decked with blue satin drapery, and furnished in a similar manner to the large saloon. The dining room has a carved oak table, which has accommodation for thirty to forty guests. It is curious to note that the backs of the oak chairs are shaped like a bishop's mitre. A beautiful green carpet, studded with groups of raised moss-roses, covers the floor of the dining-room. Mitre-shaped panels are on the walls.

A chandelier, with a hundred coloured wax candles, hangs from the splendid stained-glass roof. Besides this chandelier, there are branching candlesticks on the walls. The drapery of the doors and windows is green velvet and satin, looped up with gold tassels.

Such are the comforts and luxuries of the harems owned by the influential pashas of Egypt. Every device of art is used in the decoration of these palaces, which reflect faintly the joys that await the true believer in the Seventh Heaven. Beautiful women of other lands come gladly to share the luxuries of this indolent life, hoping to win the costly gifts that the lords of the harems bestow upon their favourites. There is no lack of candidates for the honour of consorting with a wealthy pasha or bey. In Syria, Circassia, Armenia, Italy, and Austria there are girls whose greatest ambition is to enter the harem.

Men of coloured races generally admire greatly the women of white races. Circassian women, who are perhaps the most beautiful and graceful of their sex, are highly valued in the harems of the East. Rarely an English woman resolves to become the bride of a pasha, and, rejecting her faith and all her traditions, enters the harem.

At ten years of age the girls purchased by the pasha enter the palace. The age of puberty in girls is reached in most Eastern countries at about eleven. Upon joining the houris, the novice is trained thoroughly in her duties. Various means are employed for developing and beautifying the body by means of diet, baths, and constant massage. This preparation for marriage lasts for about twelve months.

The elaborate massage gives to the skin the colour and velvety softness of a peach. Great attention is given to manicure and pedicure. The tresses are continually combed, oiled, and scented, and odorous pomades are used for the whole of the body.

Each group of six girls is attended by a young eunuch, who is instructed in his duties by an older eunuch.

Slave girls were formerly chosen in public once a year by the sovereign. A circular was published in the spring-time, announcing that about fifty girls are required from the age of twelve to eighteen. They were required to be pretty in features, well-shaped in figure, with copious, long hair. At an appointed hour the candidates assembled in an open space or market place, dressed in their finest garments.

The royal purchaser arrived upon the scene attended by his secretary, officials, several physicians and servants. One after another the eager girls were paraded under the direction of one of the principal doctors. They were ordered to display their bosoms, legs and arms, and to let loose their tresses. A severe scrutiny of the teeth followed. The girls were then commanded to stoop, walk, and show how they smiled. At a nod of their future owner's head, they were selected, and the secretary wrote down their names. The parents, who stood by, were told that the girls must be at the harem on the following morning.

Gleeful congratulations were showered upon the happy, smiling maidens who were chosen. They were complimented and flattered by their relatives and friends. The rejected damsels retired in groups, and throwing themselves on the ground, wept and groaned for their bitter misfortune. They knew that this want of success would seriously deteriorate their value.

In the future it would be difficult to remove this stigma of uncomeliness. Rich men would not want them; they were destined to marry a poor man of their own class. Not for them were the luxuries, the gifts, and the pleasures of the harem life. Consoled by their companions, they dispersed, sore at heart and crying. Very early the next morning the fortunate girls hastened to the palace and presented themselves.

CHAPTER XVII

WOMEN IN THE HAREM

IN the poetry of Arabia the most loved and admired of maidens is lithe in body and "elegant as a twig of the Oriental willow." The beauty meet for the bride of a pasha must own luxuriant hair of the deepest black. Her cheeks should be rosy in the centre, and a mole, or beauty spot, is an added charm. Blue eyes are not usually prized; the eyes should be black, large, and almond-shaped, full of yearning softness, with long, drooping lashes. The eyebrows must be arched and not thick.

A small mouth is esteemed, and the nose should be straight. Bright, ruddy lips should reveal regular, small, white teeth. The breasts must be firm, rounded, and not large. A slender waist is an essential charm, and so is a fullness of the hips. The tapering fingers should not be large, and the feet well-formed and small.

The eyes of the Oriental belle are very beautiful and expressive, and their glance is rendered more conspicuous by the veil which covers the lower features. In Andalusia, where there is a

Moorish strain in the people, the "black eye that mocks her coal-black veil" often glows with an extraordinary fascination from the white, moon-like faces of the women. Even more lambent are the glances of an Egyptian woman.

Miss Sara Jeanette Duncan, in "A Social Departure," speaks of the eyes of the women of Cairo —"conscious, tantalising eyes that shine lustrous between their blackened fringes, with a gilt wooden tube between and a good long strip of *yashmak* hanging from it, making a mystery of nose and lips and chin. They may all be beautiful —the presumption is against it, but the possibility is always there, and with crows' feet gathered too palpably above the *yashmak,* the eyes express the possibility in the most alluring manner—knowing very well that you are thinking of it, secure in the knowledge that you can't find out."

In his "Eastern Sketches" Thackeray writes of the Circassian beauties: "It is the Circassian blood, I suppose, to which the Turkish aristocracy that governs Egypt must be indebted for the fairness of their skin. Ibrahim Pasha, riding by in his barouche, looked like a bluff, jolly-faced English Dragoon officer, with a grey moustache and red cheeks, such as you might see on a field-day at Maidstone."

"The ladies whom we saw were equally fair, that is, the very slight particles of the persons of ladies which our lucky eyes were permitted to gaze on. These lovely creatures go through the town by parties of three or four, mounted on donkeys, and attended by slaves holding on at the crupper, to receive the lovely riders lest they should fall, and shouting out shrill cries of 'Schmaalek' 'Amlenck' (or however else these words may be pronounced), and flogging on the progress right and left with the buffalo-thong. But the dear creatures are even more closely disguised than at Constantinople; their bodies are enveloped with a large black silk hood, like a cab head; the fashion seemed to be to spread their arms out, and give their covering all the amplitude of which it was capable, as they beamed an ogled you from under their black masks with their big rolling eyes. The Arab women are some of the noblest figures I have ever seen. The habit of carrying jars on the head always gives the figure grace and motion, and the dress the women wear certainly displays it to full advantage."

The Persians are not so enthusiastic as the Arabs in their admiration for black eyes. They prefer gray eyes, or those that flash with the colour of red wine.

El-Sett Budur, in the "Arabian Nights," may be taken as a type of Eastern loveliness. Her hair was dark brown, and hung in three tresses that reached to her feet.

"Her cheeks are formed of an anemone divided into two corollas; they have the purple tinge of wine, and her nose is straighter and more delicate than the finest sword-blade."

"Her lips are coloured agate and coral; her tongue secretes eloquence; her saliva is more desirable than the juice of grapes."

"But her bosom, blessed be the Creator, is a living seduction. It bears twin breasts of the purest ivory, rounded, and that may be held within the five fingers of one hand."

Lane refers to the delightful moulding of the Egyptian woman's body, and says that fine forms are commoner than entirely beautiful faces. Many of the Nubian girls are extremely lovely, and willowy in figure. "Blacker is her hair than the darkness of night, blacker than the berries of the blackberry bush," runs an Egyptian inscription in the Louvre.

The older ideal of a graceful woman in Egypt was slenderness in form, resembling Psyche, or the figure of a boy. On the ancient paintings of the walls, and in statuary, it is often difficult to distinguish the men from the women. There is a strong facial likeness in the sexes even at this day.

In the time of the Ptolemys, the standard of female beauty seems to have changed, and we find in the statues a tendency to represent women as stouter in body, with curving outlines. From this period women seem to have cultivated plumpness. The chief characteristics of an Egyptian beauty were brilliant eyes, a soft skin, and a full figure. In Turkey most women desire to be fat, and they eat fattening food for that purpose. It is said that women of Eastern countries maintain the firmness of their flesh much longer than their sisters of the West.

The beards of the men in Egypt are much admired by women. A man should have a flowing beard, and a woman long hair. Herodotus states that the priests of ancient Egypt cut off their beards as a mark of sorrow and mourning. The Jews also cultivated the long beard.

Women in the harems of Cairo strive to increase the size and the brightness of their dark eyes by the use of kohl, which was a custom of the older days in Israel, and is still practised in India. To enhance the blackness and expression of the eyes Egyptian women of all classes stain the eyelids with galena. The lashes are also darkened.

EGYPTIAN GIRLS AT THEBES

The origin of veiling the faces of Mohammedan women is actually much older than the advent of Mohammed. This custom prevailed in very early times among the Arabs. In ancient Arabia men of fine and attractive countenances wore the veil as a defence against the glance of malign spirits. Havelock Ellis suggests that this may have been the source of the practice of veiling amongst women.

As clothing is frequently employed more as an erotic lure than as a protection against cold, or from reasons of modesty, it is likely that the Arab veil was adopted by women as an attraction. The domino and the veil arouse curiosity concerning the features that they conceal, just as clothing excites interest in the charms that it hides. This is proved by the fact that savage courtesans, among tribes wherein the women are nude, put on garments as a token of their calling and a lure to the eye. Undoubtedly, the Eastern veil focusses interest and curiosity upon the face.

An Eastern song sets forth the loveliness of women in these lines:—

"The complexion of my love is like the freshness of the velvet-looking jessamine; her face is as resplendent as the bright, bright moon; her lips are as rosy as the choicest wine, and her lily-white bosom the fairest and softest-looking that an amorous youth ever beheld."

"Oh! beauteous creature, the perfume of whose breath is like the grateful odour of the musk rose, allow me to sip sweets from thy ruby lips, and pour forth into thy ear the passion that consumes my heart."

The Circassian women who recruit the harems of Turkey and Egypt are the flowers of their race. Many have blue eyes and fair complexions, and their forms are exquisite. Their native costumes are perhaps unattractive to Western eyes. They are clad in baggy trousers of white staff, and a sort of dark coat that reaches from the neck almost to the ankles. A gaudy shawl is twisted about the body around the waist and loins. Their plentiful hair falls in long, thick plaits. Upon the head they wear a gauze veil.

Bodenstedt, a poet and an accredited critic of womanly beauty, declares that the Georgians are a very handsome race, but he does not consider that the women excel the men in beauty. The women's faces seemed to this writer lacking in intelligence and refinement. "In a Georgian everything fades with youth. The eyes, which, notwithstanding their apparent fire, never expressed anything but calm and voluptuous indolence, lose their lustre; the nose, which even in its normal relations exceeds the limits of beauty, assumes, in consequence of the premature hollowness of the cheeks, such abnormal dimensions that many people imagine that it actually continues to grow; and the bosom, which the national costume makes no effort to conceal, prematurely loses its natural firmness—all of which phenomena are observed in European women much less frequently, and in a less exaggerated form. If you add to this the habit, so prevalent among Georgians, young and old, of using white and red cosmetics, you will understand that such rude and inartistic arts of the toilet can only add to the observer's sense of dissatisfaction."

The wealthy owner of a seraglio often selects those Circassian women who are most susceptible to blushing. A capacity for blushing adds to a girl's monetary value in the harem market.

The custom of the women of the Abode of Bliss is to dress in their daintiest attire for the pleasure of their husbands in the home; but out-of-doors they often wear plain and unattractive clothes. When not invited to the presence of the pasha, the girls often wear dowdy, untidy costumes in the harem.

Romantic love, based upon highly refined sentiment and mutual esteem, as it is understood in the older Western nations, is perhaps rarely associated with polygamy and love in the harem. Nevertheless, in the single marriages, which are the rule amongst the greater number of Turks and Egyptians, there is often intense conjugal devotion.

In a very ancient collection of Aryan maxims, by Halâ, there are sentiments which show that the love of men and women was not wholly of the senses. A lover speaks thus: "As in sickness without a physician; as living with relatives when one is poor; as the sight of an enemy's prosperity —so is it difficult to endure separation from you."

It is easy to accept the monogamic principle in marriage as the noblest and highest form of love between the sexes, and to dismiss all possibility of lofty emotion and refined feeling from the harem marriage. I have heard more than one Western woman, living under Eastern custom, assert that polygamy possessed many advantages for their sex, and solved the problem of the enforced celibacy which is common among whole masses of women in the monogamous countries. One of these ladies professed a strong preference for "the sheltered, protected life of the women of the East."

Let us survey a part of the teaching of the apostle of the creed of Islam referring to men's relations to women. Among them we shall find several precepts that point to an esteem for the mother and wife.

First, in regard to mothers, Mohammed affirmed that "Heaven lieth at the feet of mothers."

Celibacy, which is one of the anomalies of Western civilisation, is forbidden in the saying: "Marriage is incumbent on all who possess the ability. There is no monasticism in Islam."

In the treatment of wives the Moslem is instructed to "admonish with kindness."

"Do you beat your wife as you would a slave? That you must not do."

"He is of the most perfect Moslems whose disposition is most liked by his own family."

"A virtuous wife is a man's best treasure."

Infidelity is severely censured, even if not actual, but of the imagination.

"Now the adultery of the eye is to look with an eye of desire on the wife of another; and the adultery of the tongue is to utter what is forbidden."

May we not believe that throughout the Orient the following beautiful conception of passionate love is cherished by many men and women?:—

"Four eyes met. There were changes in two souls. And now I cannot remember whether he is a man and I a woman. Or he is a woman and I a man. All I know is, there were two. Love came and there is one."

On the other hand, the segregation of women has its flagrant disadvantages. There can be no true social intercourse between the sexes, and no reciprocal understanding of each other's spiritual and mental needs and aspirations in societies wherein men and women move in entirely separate spheres. A girl entering the harem at twelve years is destined for the rest of her life, unless she deserts, to spend long indolent days in the company of her own sex.

Her sole desire is to become an *ikbal,* a petted plaything of her master, and to receive his lavish gifts and favours. The outside world scarcely exists for her. Too often she has had little or no education; she lives divorced from culture, and knows nothing of the great movements in modern thought. The dressing of her hair, the polishing of her nails, and such preservation of her external charms are her chief and constant care. She speaks to no man but the pasha and her emasculated attendants. Certain privileges are vouchsafed to her when she becomes a mother, and there is then more occupation for her energies. But so long as she is childless, the days are idle, vapid, and productive of *ennui*.

The odalisque amuses herself with childish games and diversions. She smokes the Eastern pipe, with its glass bowl and long tube, as she squats on the languorous divan. Enervated by laziness, and bored from lack of employment for brain or hands, she seeks the solace of hashish, opium, and strong liquors. The bath, massage, and dressing occupy only a small part of the day. For the rest, she merely lounges, smoking or eating sweetmeats.[1]

Hashish, or fakir's plant, produces dreaminess without loss of consciousness, and many of the inmates of the harem use it freely. After taking it a strong thirst ensues, which is quenched with sherbet or wine.

The use of perfumes of a powerful odour is common throughout Islam. Mohammed, according

[1] Thackeray refers to the alleged indecency of the women of the Cairo harems, in his "Eastern Sketches": "All their humour, my Dragoman tells me, is of the questionable sort, and a young Egyptian gentleman, son of a Pasha, whom I subsequently met at Malta, confirmed the statement, and gave a detail of the practices of private life which was anything but edifying. . . . He could give us no idea, he said, of the *wit* of the Egyptian women and their skill in *double entendre;* nor I presume, did we lose much by our ignorance."

to his favourite wife Ayesha, was very fond of the scent of musk and ambergris, and liked to smell camphor burning amongst wood. Musk is a favourite scent. It is popular in the Eastern harems, and is known as "the noblest of perfumes." Castoreum, vanilla, myrrh, otto of roses, sandal, and the perfumes from strongly-odorous flowers, such as the lily and tuberose, are all used.

Henna, used for staining the finger nails, gives forth a peculiar sweet odour. The flowers are often used in the harems to scent the body.

In spite of the religious injunction to avoid alcoholic liquors, wine is generally imbibed in the seraglios.

Under conditions in which one man controls several wives and a large regiment of concubines, it is obvious that polygamy does not solve adequately the problem of celibacy for women. Such an overplus of women for one man is an anomaly; and it is not necessary that I should be more explicit in allusion to this defect in the harem system.

CHAPTER XVIII

THE GUARDIANS OF THE SERAGLIO

A LARGE staff of overseers, nurses, and servants is necessary for the proper conduct of a rich man's harem. The autocrat, and very frequently the tyrant, of the palace is the Chief Eunuch, who directs a number of subordinate eunuchs, and supervises the whole of the servants who attend upon the wives, *ikbals,* and their lord and master, the pasha.

The profession of eunuch in Egypt is a very old one. Figures of these functionaries appear on the oldest Assyrian and Egyptian monuments. The head eunuch of antiquity was a personage of great influence in the world of the seraglio; and he seems to have been, in some cases, the confidential companion of kings and nobles, as well as the custodian of the concubines.

The royal Chief Eunuch holds an exalted position in the palace. He wears a gorgeous uniform, and is seen constantly at state ceremonies and social assemblies. In political affairs he possesses considerable influence. In all the aristocratic harems the Grand Eunuch is feared by the women and the servants, for their lives are practically in his hands.

An insubordinate or troublesome odalisque may soon find herself singled out for punishment if she offends the Chief Eunuch. It is said that eunuchs of all ranks frequently accept bribes from the women of the harems, and that some become very rich from this source. Every ambitious girl yearns to shine in the palace as an *ikbal,* and it is within the eunuch's power to assist her in this promotion from the common file to a position of high privilege.

The Chief Eunuch needs to exercise much vigilance in protecting the favourites of the pasha. Jealousy is extremely common in the harems, and all kinds of plots are hatched against the *ikbals* to bring them into disfavour with their lord. Attempts are sometimes made to poison the favourite of the pasha. Envy engenders all manner of malicious chatter and deliberate slander. The making or the undoing of an *ikbal* rests largely in the hands of the superior eunuch and those immediately beneath him in rank and influence.

In an affluent pasha's harem the highest caste among the ladies are the Kadens, the beautiful Circassians, who are especially loved by their owner. The Odalisques come next; and these women are the attendants, or maids of honour, on the pasha. The favoured woman of a brief reign is the Ikbal. When she becomes pregnant she is raised to the status of a Kaden. The Oustas are female servants of the household, who wait upon the wives and the ikbals. The Dadas are the nurses of the numerous children. Beneath all these grades are the slaves of lowly birth and of alien race.

Early in the growth of polygamy the powerful man who surrounded himself with women, purchased or captured, discovered that his wives often exhibited errant desires. Men of less influence in the community envied his good fortune in the possession of several women; and they often used means to seduce his wives from their fidelity. Romances of the harem abound in the stories of elopement, intrigue, clandestine assignations, stolen visits to the palace by night, the forcible abduction of ikbals, and the murder of eunuchs and guards by hired bravos and professional stranglers.

A pasha lives, like the mediæval baron of England, in a fortified palace, or castle, with men-at-arms for the protection of his personal property. The armed eunuch came into existence as a necessary defence against the men who coveted the wives of their more fortunate neighbours. It was essential also that the women should be closely watched and kept under lock and key, for the human nature of women is like that of men, subject to variability in love, and apt to revolt against the strictest domestic conventions.

Now, a normal man, placed in guardianship of a number of young and charming women, is naturally exposed to very palpable temptation. In a word, he was not considered a safe chaperon and overseer. The risks of his defection from his responsible duties must be reduced as much as possible. He must be deprived of his masculinity.

Boys are dedicated to this profession from birth, and many of them aspire to enter this service. It is said that even to-day young boys of colour are sometimes abducted when the demand for more eunuchs arises. In other cases they are purchased by the Chief Eunuch and handed over to the surgeon.

The effect of emasculation must be noted, for it is of importance in a study of harem life. That the operation fails to achieve its chief purpose is fairly well known. Women of the seraglios have been known to elope with eunuchs and to marry them.

The result upon the secondary sexual characters are several, and very marked. There is a change in structure and appearance. The legs tend to lengthen; and in Cairo eunuchs are often recognised in crowds by their height. It is not true that the emasculated man is always dwarfed in stature. The voice becomes high-pitched and penetrating. From the musical point of view the Italian professional castrati, among singers, possess exceptionally beautiful voices.

Generally speaking, the male characteristics are lessened and modified. The guardians of the harem are often dull, inactive, and effeminate in their habits. Some tend to obesity. It is doubtful whether the moral qualities suffer to the extent that is usually believed. But it is stated that many of these neuter men are exceedingly sly, cunning, and perfidious.

It is generally believed that eunuchs are lacking in courage, and that they show certain docile, timorous, and cowardly traits. This has, however, been denied in some instances. The guardians of the harems are reputed to be extremely cruel. This attribute may derive from their changed physical qualities, but it is probably a normal manifestation of Oriental indifference to suffering and the stoicism long inculcated by precept and example.

An Egyptian will flog a servant until he faints. Many are the accounts of Eastern severity and excessive callousness to the pain endured by others. Torture still exists in several parts of the East as a corrective and a penalty for crime.

I know the English wife of an eminent Moor, who related to me her sensations of horror and indignation when she saw her husband cruelly thrash a slave-boy, on the bare back, with a cane until the blood flowed. She could not reconcile this utter indifference in the infliction of suffering upon a helpless servant with her husband's conjugal tenderness and his kindness to his own children.

The imperturbability that the Oriental often displays in the contemplation of pain, and the commission of acts that appear to us as grossly cruel, is a subject of great psychological interest and importance.

"About the only good and conspicuous virtue that we possess in England," said to me an ex-minister of the Church, "is our kindness and consideration towards animals." In the Mohammedan religion the believer is enjoined to show kindness to brutes and clemency for slaves. Nevertheless, the counsel is frequently, and indeed commonly, set aside when anger is aroused. And apparently much of the cruelty of the East is purposive and carefully devised.

The source of Oriental apathy in relation to

pain, and the seeming enjoyment in inflicting physical suffering arises probably from a certain obtuseness of the nerves. When we see the fakirs of Cairo, and elsewhere, walking with bare feet upon bayonet points, and otherwise injuring and mutilating the flesh, as an exhibition of stoicism, we have a marked instance of the Eastern capacity for enduring pain. He who stands torments without an outcry is often unsympathetic at the spectacle of another man's manifest bodily anguish, and may even derive pleasure from witnessing the effect of pain.

Physiologically, the Eastern people show an aptitude for the personal toleration and the infliction of suffering. Pain is the common lot; it must be endured by oneself and imposed upon others. Fatalistic doctrines foster the personal endurance of physical and mental travails. That which is must be suffered uncomplainingly.

Cruelty loses its Western connotation in most parts of Africa and Asia. It was the humane, cultured, and artistic Moors who introduced bullfighting into Spain. To-day, in Northern Africa, and in several parts of Asia, one does not expect to find any conception of kindness to animals as it is practised in many Western societies. In Spain, the Morisco influence has, no doubt, some relation to the callous treatment of horses and other domestic animals. The Spaniard, who treats his wife and children with tender affection, may show a callous disregard for the suffering of his horse or mule.

Probably the women of Egypt expect a certain amount of harshness and physical force on the part of husbands. In variable forms we observe this predilection for the aggressive, forceful man among a vast number of women of the Western civilisations. The rôle of woman in love is more or less passive, actual or assumed, and in spite of the denials of some of the advanced feminists, many women like to realise masculine superiority in the matter of muscular strength. Some women even court and demand subordination at the hands of the men.

Marriage by capture, in modern primitive communities, is frequently a mere burlesque of ancient abduction. But the women would not be content if their suitors showed no roughness; and they simulate resistance by scratching, kicking and biting. Among the Bedouins of to-day, the bride is carried away forcibly by the bridegroom and his "best men." The girl resists stoutly, often wounding the young men with stones. It is her full intention to marry her captor, but she must keep up the fashion of resistance. And the more she kicks, bites, and scratches, the more is she esteemed by her friends, and presumably by her husband.

Sometimes an Arab bride will resist her husband after the ceremony, when established in his tent as duly wedded. In such cases, she expects to be beaten, and there is reason to suppose that she likes chastisement.

In the Indian Kama Sutra there are directions for whipping women, and the women, though they raise protests, would be surprised, and probably disappointed, if the husband failed to recognise the time-honoured custom. "A dear one's blows hurt not long." "The Perfumed Garden" of the Arabs contains several allusions to castigation.

Western morality regards such chastisement with reprobation and horror. Let us remember that, in certain very significant directions, the Orientals excel us in the art of love, and especially in their desire to charm and please women. The blunt, matter-of-fact British lover—who, though good-natured enough, is often devoid of delicacy and an understanding of women's natures—is not a very successful wooer in the East. Many Hindu women are extremely candid when discussing the difference between the Western men and those of their own race.

Not three hundred years ago we thrashed women

publicly in the streets of London. Gentlewomen flogged their maid-servants, apparently with zest; and Judge Jeffreys, in sentencing a woman to be scourged, charged the hangman to ply the whip "till her blood runs down." Even nowadays, in England, women, and especially children, are often beaten with extreme cruelty. As evidence we may inspect the museum of torture instruments formed by the Society for the Prevention of Cruelty to children.

The infliction of pain upon others is associated with rites of self-mortification, penance, and pious fasting. In all religions that prescribe self-imposed torture we shall find an indifference to pain cultivated as a tradition. And such capacity for enduring painful penances explains, in part, the lack of sensitivity in causing bodily suffering to one's dependents, or to heretics and delinquents.

The severities formerly meted by the eunuchs to offenders in the household were said to be ferocious.

CHAPTER XIX

HAREM INTRIGUES AND SCANDALS

POLYGAMY, as exemplified by the harem system, favours intrigue. Even the *ikbal* of a great and influential pasha, though much petted and lavishly endowed with money and fine jewels, often sighs for a real and romantic love affair. She may have entered the harem at a tender age, knowing very little indeed of the needs of her heart and dormant emotional nature. Her owner may show her much favour and kindness, and treat her with a courteous respect. And yet discontent and restlessness assail her. She may loathe the very hand that caresses her.

While the rulers of the harem exercise the most cautious and elaborate selection in the purchase of their mistresses, no such choice is open to the woman. Sold in childhood, they enter married life without any experience of men. No wonder that harems are often hotbeds of intrigue between the inmates and the outside world.

It may be urged that under monogamic marriage thousands of women experience dissatisfaction with their chosen partners, and suffer a terrible ennui from conjugality. At all events, the woman of a monogamous nation is able to exercise very considerable free choice, and even before the strictest marriage of convenience, arranged as in France, the plighted girl is allowed to meet her future husband in society. The maiden destined for the harem has not this opportunity. She goes to an union with an utterly unknown man, who may be morally and physically repulsive to her.

The wife of the average shopkeeper and artisan in Egypt has, of course, rather more freedom of selection. She is not brought from a foreign country, and condemned to a kind of gilded durance amid a number of women. We must not forget that a large proportion of the population of the East are practically, if not always, quite strictly monogamous.

For the present we are concerned with the life of the women of the harem, and their specific temptations to inconstancy. Let it be remembered that, from racial causes, and the sensuous atmosphere in which they are reared, these women are peculiarly susceptible to passion. Their whole thought is concentrated upon love and its pleasures. In the state of hyperæsthesia thus set up, it is not strange that they should brood incontinently, and long for experiences denied to them in the seraglio.

Does not every ardent woman yearn for a great passion? Polygamy does not expel the polyandrous instinct from a woman's breast. A psychic craving for a true heart-mate may dominate an inmate of the harem. She demands a love that she cannot secure under polygamy. Often, no doubt, her restlessness and spirit of rebellion springs from lack of occupation for the mind.

A measure of liberty is accorded to the woman of the Egyptian harems. Once a year they may leave the Abode of Bliss for a few weeks, and, under a certain amount of supervision, mingle with the world. They are, of course bound to wear the veil, and to observe the ordinary conventions governing the conduct of their sex in public places.[1] Freed for a spell, and filled with a spirit of adventure, the girl walks the fashionable promenades of Cairo.

In the cosmopolitan throng, ever going and coming in the glaring thoroughfares, the beauty from the harem paces, observed for her grace and the irresistible challenge of her deep eyes. It is not difficult to find an excuse for a sudden uplifting of the veil. A mosquito may have stung her cheek;

[1] A friend just returned from Egypt informs me that the upper class women now wear transparent veils, and that some have discarded them entirely.

a fly may tickle her nose. At the instant when the veil is swiftly raised, a handsome young Englishman, American, or Frenchman may chance to pass. It is, of course, a mere accident that a man should pass by at that moment. The glance is enough; the flame from those languishing eyes, the witching smile of the curved, ruddy lips, showing a treasure of pearly teeth, and the delicate ivory of the complexion, touched with a rosy pink, have aroused throbbing emotions in the breast of the young man.

In this enchanted region of mystery and romance, elusive, seductive, incomprehensible Egypt, the young and adventure-loving stranger is prone to speculate closely upon the womanly loveliness immured behind the formidable barriers of the harem. He longs to emulate the exploits of Don Juan, who, in spite of bar and padlock, contrived to enter the sanctum of a royal seraglio. He recalls the lines of Byron upon "a thousand bosoms there beating for love, as the cag'd birds for air."

"A bride from the harem"; the words ring with romance. The visitor retraces his footsteps. His eyes are dazzled, and aching for another glance at those exquisite features. Again he encounters the fair Georgian, and may be this time her eyes subtly express the agitation of her heart. She, too, is fascinated. It is not the first time that she has glanced covertly at the broad-shouldered, attractive young tourist.

The spell is cast. These two are secretly enamoured. They wish to converse; they long to be alone. But a whisper in Cairo is heard a mile away. Spies lurk everywhere; they seem to hover invisibly in the air. One is never safe from them. The crafty eunuchs do not lose sight of their charge. She is watched by vigilant eyes, dogged by unseen hirelings, who hold her very life in their keeping. Even a gleam from her eyes may betray her to her custodians. Her look should be demure and downcast.

Tingling with curiosity and assailed by tyrannous desire, the stranger waits the next day, in the hope of snatching an answering flash from those peerless eyes. He is rewarded. But his triumph is marred by the approach of a dark-visaged, sullen guardian, who eyes him with a smile of cruel menace. He is an eunuch. Is this creature bribable? The young adventurer has heard of elopements from the harem, aided by the guards. He returns the eunuch's leer with a significant expression. He is now bent upon the conquest and abduction of the lovely Georgian, whose image is before him by day and night.

These things are done. By a contest in wily methods, the would-be champion and deliverer of the damsel succeeds in parleying unseen with her dusky spy. The man's palm itches for baksheesh. Probably he loves a girl in the harem, and he would like to escape with her to a far corner of the country, or to a foreign land, and make her his wife. Allah has given many women to the rich. He needs money for his project. Even if he has no such plot concealed in his innermost bosom, he still loves baksheesh. Remember his life is in peril. The price must be high, if he is to abet in this daring business.

In spite of his cupidity, the lover rewards the eunuch to the full. No sum is too high a price for the winning of the beautiful Georgian maiden.

One day the girl is missed from the pasha's harem. The Chief Eunuch is distracted; his subordinates tremble. There is an inquiry. Probably there is the mysterious disappearance of an eunuch about the same time. Outside of the harem little or nothing is heard of the scandal. A week or so afterwards there is a quiet wedding in Paris between a wealthy young Frenchman and a charming lady of foreign extraction.

The kidnapping of men into the harem is contrived by the eunuchs at the instigation, and through the heavy bribery, of intrepid ladies suffering from extreme boredom. Wise persons in the East do not ask questions. Whatever happens, no matter how strange or staggering on the senses, do not say anything. Pass on as though nothing had happened out of the common course of daily affairs. Men go into the alleys. They are seen no more. Apparently the earth has gaped and swallowed them. If they chance to be personages of small importance there is no hue and cry, no quest. "East is East."

Miss Emmeline Lott, who dedicates her book on "Harem Life," written in 1865, to "His Highness Ismael Pacha, Viceroy of Egypt," makes some astounding statements concerning the mysterious poisonings, sudden deaths, and tragedies that happened in the harems in which she lived as a governess. I have no desire to make over-statements; on the contrary, I wish to approach the question of the status of women under polygamy with an open and impartial mind. I imagine, however, that Miss Lott would scarcely have dedicated her book to the Viceroy had it contained questionable statements or exaggerations.

This lady recounts several instances of cruelty practised upon slaves and women. She is explicit in her charge that the eunuchs conspire to introduce men to the harems, and she relates how she witnessed a saturnalia of men and slave girls after dark on a moonlight night.

"I had heard much and read a great deal about the impossibility of men entering the harems of the East, considered as 'sacred' by all Moslems; that not a true believer has ever been known to visit the 'Abode of Bliss' of a true Mussulman. But now that I had seen the female slaves of the harem rambling about at night with the eunuchs, the guardians of these girls, and other muffled figures, I could not help giving credence to the assertion of a celebrated writer on Oriental life that, crabbed and cross-grained as the eunuchs may be, still there are many of them who bow the knee to the sovereign ruler of Egypt, Prince Baksheesh, and that golden keys do sometimes throw back the rusty hinges of the doors they guard, or else how came the slaves and their partners, those muffled figures?"

CHAPTER XX

THE ARABIAN CONCUBINATE

THE early Arabs, a fierce, militant race, became, through conquests in India, Persia and Spain, a powerful and civilising force from the seventh to the tenth centuries. Before their expansion they were nomadic shepherds, wresting a poor substance from a sterile soil. In the height of their prosperity the Arabs excelled in the sciences, in medicine, in the arts and in philosophy, and built up a mighty civilisation.

The town dwellers in modern Arabia are sometimes polygamous, but the mass of the wandering herdsmen and traders marry only one wife. About a hundred years ago plural marriage was as comparatively uncommon in Arabia as it is to-day.

Pinkerton, in his "Voyages and Travels," 1811, states that the Bedouins were mostly monogamists, though a few had two wives. In these cases the women were supervisors of the husband's affairs during his absence, or one would travel with him on trading expeditions, while the other remained in charge at home.

In this country, as elsewhere, the harem is the luxury of the wealthy. Polygamy is declining in Arabia, as it is in Turkey; but in Mecca, the rich sometimes maintain two or three wives and a number of mistresses. According to Burckhardt, some of the middle-class Arabs used to buy young Abyssinian girls, keep them as concubines, and often sell them to foreigners.

In ancient times a custom known as *beena* marriage was common in Arabia. The wife was the actual owner of her tent and household goods, and could leave her husband upon just cause. There is no doubt that the Arabs have always tended to respect a woman's rights regarding property, and this respect has favoured the position of women, especially since the coming of Mohammed, who laid down definite laws.

Mut'ah marriage, still surviving in Arabia and Persia, is a curious form of temporary alliance, and is of ancient origin. Letourneau refers to this union as mot'a. R. Smith, in "Kinship," alludes to it. The woman remains in her own home, but becomes a temporary wife on payment to her of a fixed amount. Sometimes the union becomes permanent; but if the wife wishes to leave the husband at the end of the agreed period, she possesses full liberty to do so. After the transient conjugal

AN ARAB WOMAN

life, a woman is free to form another mut'ah marriage. Mohammed did not sanction this marriage, and it was abolished at a later date. But it is apparently still known in some parts of Arabia. Letourneau says that mut'ah unions were practised by the ancient Hebrews.[1]

Some writers seem anxious to prove that Arab polygamy and concubinage are commonly practised, and that the women are in a condition of slavery. There is, however, conclusive evidence that the nomadic Arabs are mostly monogamous; also that their women exercise considerable influence and possess clearly-defined rights. Arabian poetry contains many laudatory tributes to the fidelity, gentleness, and courage of women.

Pinkerton noted very little difference between Moslem and Christian marriage. He states that the women of Arabia "seem to be as free and happy as those of Europe can possibly be." Divorce, says Pinkerton, was rarely undertaken without the most stringent reasons, repudiation being considered a dishonourable proceeding, because it casts a stigma on the wife and her relatives. The writer observes further that the women seemed to have much liberty, and often a high degree of power in the family and the group.

[1] Letourneau *op. cit.*

The townspeople who kept harems were urged more by social vanity than by sensuality. Pinkerton says that the women of the seraglios were not guarded by eunuchs; in fact, there were then no eunuchs in Arabia. But Sir Richard Burton alludes in two or three passages to eunuchs in modern Arabia. Pinkerton asserts that the Arabs strongly disapproved of castration.

Burton, in his "Pilgrimage to Al-Madinah and Meccah," relates that while staying in the house of the Shayk Hamid he never saw any women but the slaves. Those girls were shy, and usually covered their faces while they talked to him. Slave girls could be bought for about £60, and the Abyssinians were the most highly valued among the women of colour. The Circassians were worth £100 to £400.

Yet it is amongst the wandering, adventurous Arabs that we must look for the birth of the ideals of romantic love and chivalry. These sons of the desert, who have been unjustly charged with cruelty to women, were, even in early times, very ardent and tender lovers. Sir Richard Burton says that men will die for love in the East. The passionate, imaginative Bedouins are mostly chivalrous in their conduct towards women. They are still gentlemen, retaining strong, lasting traditions of honour, courtesy and hospitality.

The Bedouin women are lithe and active. Arabs dislike fat persons. As a rule, the women are unveiled, though they wear a head covering. Burton describes some of the beauties of the plains as extremely handsome. The Bedouins do not only esteem the women for their bodily attractions. There is a real sentiment of conjugal love, and both husband and wife lament partings, if only for a few months. On the return of the husband, the wife greets him with cries of delight.

Ages ago the women of Arabia were "a race of heroines." We cannot suppose that the spirit of those days is dead; that Arabian poets do not voice the emotions of living men, and that the Arab lover of to-day looks upon his bride, or his concubine, as a mere serf. Men do not languish, lapse into despair, and commit suicide for the simple possession of slaves. Yet Letourneau is inclined to class the Arabs with barbarians.

A form of capture-marriage is practised among the Bedouins. The girl is wooed and her consent secured; but she must flee from her suitor and assume a defensive attitude, in accordance with ancient convention. Sometimes she hides coyly from her lover, and is provided with food by her relatives. In one tribe the bride is protected by her women friends, but she allows herself to be caught and carried to the bridegroom's tent.

It is curious to note the pains taken by some writers to underrate the refinement of sentiment in love among races practising polygamy. Conjugal affection, as I have endeavoured to show in these pages, is not incompatible with plural marriage. Burckhardt, who is often quoted by Professor Westermarck, says that he doubts whether the Arabs ever mean anything but "the grossest animal desire" when they talk of the passion of love. Westermarck often allows his monogamic bias to colour his inquiry into polygamy. But Sir Richard Burton is more dispassionate. He quotes Sonnini, who, by the way, was no great admirer of Egypt.[2]

This writer speaks of "the generous virtues, the example of magnanimity and affectionate attachment, the sentiments ardent, yet gentle, forming a delightful unison with personal charms in the harems of the Mamluks."

Pinkerton discerned but little difference in the marriage of Christians and Mohammedans; Mrs. Garnett thinks the women of Turkey are, in the main, quite as happy as the women of England;

[2] *Op. cit.*

and apparently Miss Margaret Noble would not exchange the life of a Hindu woman for that of an emancipated English sister.

It may be urged that the tending towards equality of the sexes among the Bedouins is attributable to the fact that they are, for the greater number, monogamous. That may be so. But polygamy is not condemned, and would probably be practised more widely were it not for the poverty of these nomads.

The Bedouins are not a religious people. Nominally they are Mohammedans, but they are not strictly devout. They observe the rule of circumcision and a few other Moslem rites. Their marriage ceremony is simple. Sons are married as soon as the father can afford the bride-price.

The system of concubinage existing in Arabia is a survival of the militarist days, when women were taken captives in battle. It is, in a sense, "free marriage." Letourneau, in "The Evolution of Marriage," writes: "If we interrogate all races, all epochs, and all countries, we see that the concubinate and concubinage have flourished, and still flourish, by the side of legal marriage."

Sir Samuel Baker was told by an Arab chief that he owned four wives. When one grew old, he "replaced her with a young one." He made four marks with a stick in the sand, saying, "This one carries water; that grinds the corn; this makes the bread; the last does not do much, as she is the youngest and my favourite."

Jealousy often exists between wives and concubines. A young girl is purchased as a slave, and her youth and comeliness allure her master. She has been "gazed upon," and in due time she becomes a paramour. The legal wife, or one of the wives, conceives a hatred for this rival, and a plot may be concocted for the slave girl's ruin.

Palgrave offers the strongest evidence that the itinerant Arabs have always accorded the virtues of courage and loyalty to their women. The tribes that are led by women-soldiers have a high estimation of the capacity of women, and among the Arabs there were many fair warriors and leaders. Often a maiden of good birth rode at the head of an army, mounted upon a camel.

It is erroneous, therefore, to associate invariably the total subjection of women with communities practising polygamy and concubinage.

CHAPTER XXI

THE WOMEN OF PERSIA

THE realm of the Shah is a reputed paradise for women. There is probably less feminine discontent in Persia than in any other country, East or West. It has often been said that where polygamy prevails women have few liberties and little influence. In this book I have adduced sufficient evidence to prove that such a view often arises from hasty preconception and from the prejudice of the Western mind against legal plural marriage and sanctioned concubinage.

Polygamy in Persia does not seem oppressive towards women, for they exercise much social and domestic power. Within the limits of their traditions, and in accord with their personal aspirations, the women of Persia, among the upper classes, are cultured, and even advanced, from the Oriental point of view.

Ancient Persian romances and poetry testify to the esteem and devotion shown by men to wives and lovers; and the old histories tell of noble women who have led armies to victory. The most passionate of love poems have been written by

Persians. Mothers in Persia are greatly honoured, and exert potent sway in the family; and grandmothers are even more venerated.[1] Mr. W. S. Landor, in "Across Coveted Lands," says that women among the Persians have great influence over men, both in political and commercial affairs. He adds that the wives are almost always the intimate friends and counsellors of their husbands. The interests in married life are mutual.

Before examining the marriage customs and social position of Persian women, let us inquire concerning the physical traits of these much-loved and eloquently-lauded houris. Dr. C. J. Wills, who lived for many years among the people of Persia, describes the women as generally dark, with full-moon faces, and fine eyes.[2] Their long hair is plaited, and often stained red, a colour much admired by the Persians, but not by most Orientals. Cosmetics and pigments for the cheeks are used somewhat freely, and the arch of the eyebrows is accentuated.

Mr. W. S. Landor[3] says that the women are of fair height, and rather inclined to stoutness of the figure. Many are fair-skinned, and all have

[1] "In the Land of the Lion and the Sun," Dr. C. J. Wills.

[2] *Op. cit.*

[3] "Across Coveted Lands."

GEORGIAN DANCING GIRLS

beautiful and expressive eyes, with arched eyebrows.

The following is an appraisement of Persian loveliness by Shereef-Eddin Romi, quoted by Havelock Ellis[4]:—

The cultivation of physical beauty is an important part of a Persian girl's education, and the standard of bodily perfection is somewhat exacting. Nevertheless, as several travellers testify,

[4] "Psychology of Sex" series, "Sexual Selection in Man," Havelock Ellis.

"A Persian treatise on the figurative terms relating to beauty shows that the hair should be black, abundant, and wavy, the eyebrows dark and arched. The eyelashes also must be dark, and like arrows from the bow of the eyebrows. There is, however, no insistence on the blackness of the eyes. We hear of four varieties of eye: the dark grey eye (or narcissus eye); the narrow elongated eye of Turkish beauties; the languishing or love-intoxicated eye; and the wine-coloured eye. Much stress is laid on the quality of brilliancy. The face is sometimes described as brown, but more especially as white and rosy. There are many references to the down on the lips which is described as greenish (sometimes bluish) and compared to herbage. This down and that on the cheeks and the stray hairs near the ears were regarded as very great beauties. A beauty spot on the chin, cheek or elsewhere were also greatly admired and evoked many poetic comparisons. The mouth must be very small. In stature a woman must be tall and erect, like the cyprus or the maritime pine. While the Arabs admired the rosiness of the legs and thighs, the Persians insisted on white legs and compared them to silver and crystal."

facial loveliness and symmetry of form are not the sole attractions. Very frequently a plain woman, possessed of sprightliness and amiability, is more cherished by a husband than the veritable belle who lacks humour and intelligence. The favourite wife is often unattractive in features and ungainly in body.

Bathing is an elaborate ritual and an ancient institution of the country. Prolonged and constant ablutions are, as we have seen, a common practice in most Mohammedan communities. In Persia women are as much addicted to hot bathing as the Turkish women. The bath-house is like a club, a place of social resort; and women spend several hours, or the greater part of the day, steeping themselves in hot water, undergoing massage and friction, and lounging on divans in warm chambers. The bath is a principal rendezvous for the women of fashion in the higher classes.

Bathing is an almost painful process in Persia and Afghanistan, and foreigners shrink from the immersion in scalding water, the hot douches, and the drastic pounding and pinching of the flesh. The operation leaves those unaccustomed to it in a state of limp enervation.

Persian ladies demand of their husbands sufficient pin-money to pay for frequent baths, and a refusal to comply would be regarded as unkindness.[5] In the bathing-houses women associate freely; they gossip, eat sweetmeats, and smoke. One of the chief diversions is drawing figures and devices upon the body with a kind of pencil. Hours are spent in this recreation. The moon, the stars, shapes of animals and birds, and the forms of trees are drawn on the bosom and the upper part of the abdomen.[6]

Music, singing and dancing are favourite amusements of Persian women. Many of them excel in relating romances of love and adventure, and in reciting the old poems and amorous songs. There is much gaiety and childish light-heartedness among the women of the harems.

Dr. C. J. Wills says that Persian women are virtuous, economical, and cleanly in their persons and in the home. They "do all they can to make home happy," and as a consequence the wife is idolised by her husband and adored by her children.[7] Their chief faults are, perhaps, a love of tittle-tattle, a tendency to quarrel among them-

[5] If the husband refuses to make the wife a fair allowance for baths and entertainments, she may take what money she can find in the house, and it is proper if she bites and scratches her spouse till he pays the pocket-money.

[6] Porter's "Travels in Persia."

[7] *Op. cit.*

selves, and jealousy. But the average family lives happily in an atmosphere of affection, and often extreme devotion.

The ritual of union is instructive, as showing the power of the wife. On the bridal night the husband is seated by the side of the bride. The right leg of the bride is placed on the left leg of the husband, and her right hand is placed upon the hand of her husband, to *show that she ought always to have the upper hand of her spouse.*

Mirza Abu Taleb, a Persian writer, is very explicit in laying down rules for husbands. A man is ordered to give his wife money without stint, or her colour will fade, her cheeks become as saffron, and she will languish and pine. If she dies of grief, through her husband's meanness, harsh treatment, or neglect, her blood will be on his head. In the day of judgment the woman will claim from the man that which he has failed to provide for her. Even the day-labourer must give all his wages to his wife. Very considerable laxity is allowed to Persian women in the matters of fasting, ritual, and penance. A wife must have all the enjoyments and recreations that a husband can reasonably provide for her. It is often said the women in the East are at best the spoilt playthings of men. This is scarcely true of Persian women. Their ascendency in the home, in business affairs, and, to a certain extent, in society is beyond question.

The mother in Persia has almost supreme authority, and the wife is, in many respects, more than equal with the husband.

"The glories of the bride," writes Dr. Wills, "pale in the strong rays of the mother of the son of the house." In this country, as in the East generally, the mother of the heir is especially honoured; but the highest respect is shown to all women who have borne children. The mothers direct all the fortunes of the sons. They select their wives. There is, however, free choice for the maidens. A girl can refuse a suitor three times. If she accepts him, he is bound to pay her a suitable marriage settlement. There is little or no courtship, as we understand it in the West. The lover looks at his chosen bride through an aperture in the room.

The marriage celebration is made the occasion for music, dancing, and feasting. Mr. W. S. Landor says that there is also a betrothal ceremony of a somewhat splendid character. Many guests are invited to these protracted festivities. The girl is congratulated by her relations and friends. She is decked in her loveliest garments, her hair adorned, her eyes darkened artificially. Attention is fixed almost wholly upon her; she is the queen of the hour, and little interest is shown in the bridegroom, who appears awkward and bashful.

During Dr. Wills' long stay in Persia, he only heard of one tragedy in conjugal life. Generally speaking, women in the *anderuns* are good friends one with another, and the trusted *confidantes* of their husbands and children.[8]

Dr. Wills states that women in Persia begin to show signs of age at forty; but Mr. W. S. Landor says that the menopause does not manifest itself until about fifty.

When walking in the streets the women are closely veiled with the *chudder*. Social intercourse with men is restricted in this country, and such interdiction is one of the principal disabilities of women.

On the other hand, women in Persia possess many rights and a number of privileges. James Atkinson, in "Customs and Manners of the Women of Persia," refers to an ancient code in which the liberties of women are clearly defined. A woman can always attend the public bath alone. She is allowed to visit her father, brother, sister, or son when she chooses, and her husband cannot force

[8] "Persia as it Is," Dr. C. J. Wills.

his company upon her on such occasions. Such intrusion would be considered unpardonable rudeness. No husband is to enter his wife's apartments without her consent or invitation. A wife may entertain her friends in her own apartments, and engage musicians and dancers to delight her guests.

When a husband enters his wife's chambers he is a visitor, and he possesses no authority over her servants. Her children and her slaves obey her, and not her spouse. The Persians assert that their women have more power and liberty than the women of Europe and the West generally. This was the opinion of Mirza Abu Taleb Khan after a visit to England.

A Persian wife is permitted by custom to tease her husband, and to indulge her humours and caprices to her heart's content. She believes that her compliance must be won, and not enforced harshly. The submissive wife often loses favour in the husband's eyes; therefore the astute Persian woman cultivates the art of pique, and shows her displeasure in little spiteful speeches and acts. A dutiful husband must wait upon his wife when she is going a journey to visit her relatives or friends. After the visit he must go to escort her back to the home, and sometimes the lady refuses to accompany him. She changes her mind suddenly, and expresses her intention of remaining longer.

In that case, the husband cannot oblige her to return. He must come again and again until the recalcitrant wife decides to accompany him.

These devices to retain a husband's love by annoying him appear rather farcical; but in Persia there is a method in a wife's management of her spouse; and apparently such uncertainty and variability are accepted by some men as the proper and normal traits of women.

Westermarck quotes Dr. Polak to show that Persian wives suffer deep pain when supplanted by another woman. No doubt such jealousy is not very infrequent; but we have the authority of other writers, to whom I have referred, that on the whole the life of the *anderun* is peaceful, and that the women are usually good friends.

As I have said before, Professor Westermarck's disapproval of polygamy blinds him to facts which prove that there are certain domestic advantages for women in polygamous societies.

Dr. Polak declares that the love extolled by the Persian poets has "either a symbolic or a very profane meaning"; in fine, it is asserted by several authorities, cited in "The History of Human Marriage," that the Oriental peoples have no conception of the romantic love of the West.

I cannot sympathise with such special pleading. Without offering any apology whatever for plural marriage, one may expose dispassionately all sides of the question, good and evil. The prime error of the writers who champion monogamy, when describing Eastern life, is their invariable tendency to rank all Mohammedans, Hindus, and the greater number of Buddhists as polygamists. We have seen that in all the countries where plurality of wives and the maintenance of concubines are sanctioned, the great bulk of the population live in monogamy.

Surely, when one hears the personal testimony of devout Mohammedan and Hindu men and women, and that of English friends who have lived in the East, one hesitates before making such wide generalisations concerning the Oriental incapacity for psychic, or spiritual, love between the sexes. In Turkey, in India, in Burma, and in Persia love is not merely "the grossest animal desire." It is quite impossible to accept such an estimate after reading the love poetry of these nations and the records of unbiassed travellers.

Who can assert truly that the beautiful poems of conjugal love by Tagore are simple poems of sensuality? In regard to Indian love, are we to dismiss the tributes of Dr. Ananda Coomaraswamy, Miss Margaret Noble, Mrs. Steele, Laurence Hope, and a number of English men and women who have lived among the Hindu people? There is no question that ages ago, in the great civilisations of the East, the love of man for woman was associated with the deepest religious emotions.

Long before Western culture, in remote eras, married love was an idyl in Egypt, Arabia and India. Reverence was shown towards women. In the lines of an ancient Hindu poet, we find such sentiments as this:—

> "Woman is man's better half,
> Woman is man's bosom friend,
> Woman is redemption's source,
> From woman springs the liberator."

What higher praise has been bestowed upon woman? The poet sings: "Women are the friends of the solitary—they solace him with their sweet converse; like to a father, in discharge of duty, consoling as a mother in misfortune."

Mercenary association of the sexes was abhorred in ancient Persia, and regarded as an abominable sin. In modern times prostitution is somewhat on the increase in the cities, and is accompanied by the usual evils.[9]

The teaching of chastity is explicit in the moral codes of Persia.

In one of the Sacred Books, it is stated: "This is the wickedest deed that hostile men do, when they keep girls away from marriage, and leaving them long without husbands, prevent them bearing children."

[9] Mr. W. S. Landor. *Op. cit.*

CHAPTER XXII

THE PERSIAN ANDERUN

THE ancient Persians were a militant race, holding sway in the East of Asia and China. They subdued Egypt, and they spread westwards into Greece. In an early epoch they were cultured, and distinguished for their knowledge of astronomy and for their poetry. In A.D. 651 Persia was conquered by the Saracens, and about a century later Khouli-Khan led an army into India and laid the land waste.

Since the Fifteenth Century the country has been ruled by Shahs, who have lived in high state and grandeur. Most of the rulers in recent times have been friendly towards England, and one monarch visited our country some years ago. The religion of Persia is a form of Mohammedanism, but there are a considerable number of Armenian residents professing Christianity.

Extravagance on the part of the majority of the Shahs has caused discontent and trouble from time to time during the past ten years.

The capital, Teheran, has a population of 210,000. The Shah maintains a harem here, and also in other towns, containing a host of concubines, but he has only one legal wife.

Dr. Wills tells us that slavery in the Persian harems is an easy existence, and that the women rarely yearn for freedom. They are very well fed and clothed, and have but little work to perform. Many of the women of the *anderun* live to a ripe old age, and have no wish to leave the establishment. Kind treatment of harem women and servants is the general rule. It is worthy of note that the Persians are kinder to animals than is the custom of most Oriental people.

The women most valued as servants are Abyssinians and Somalis. According to Dr. Wills [1] girls of from twelve to fourteen years of age are worth about £40 in purchase money; while damsels of lighter colour are often worth from £80 to £100. The very dark negroes are much less valuable.

The separate apartment system prevails in the harems, each beauty possessing sole rights over her quarters and her attendants. Only a few eunuchs are kept in this country, which goes to prove a greater freedom than most women enjoy in the life of the seraglio. The women are often excellent friends of each other, and on the au-

[1] "In the Land of the Lion and the Sun."

thority of English writers, discord is infrequent.

The proportion of polygamous marriages in Persia has been set down as five per cent., or even two per cent., of the population. Probably concubinage is more widely spread than recognised plural marriage, but polygamy is certainly the exception and not the rule.

A book of Persian maxims on women proclaims:—

"Be that man's life immersed in gloom
Who weds more wives than one.
With one his cheeks retain their bloom,
His voice a cheerful tone;
These speak his honest heart at rest
And he and she are always blest;
But when with two he seeks for joy,
Together they his soul annoy.
With two no sunbeam of delight
Can make his day of misery bright."

Punishment will be meted out, therefore, to husbands who have acted unjustly or unkindly towards their wives. A husband must think always of his wife's welfare, and strive to please her in all things great and small. When he goes to the market he should buy her a gift of fruit and carry it home to her to show that he thinks of her pleasure. When the wife goes on a journey the husband must escort her. If she wishes her women visitors to remain in the house all night, she may give them couches in her chamber, and the husband must sleep alone.

Infractions of this somewhat exacting code for husbands can be remedied by the woman suing for separation. Divorce for men is not easy in Persia; in spite of Mohammedan legal provision, the process is difficult. It is easier for a woman to divorce her partner.

The evanescence of a husband's ardour is a grievous matter, and the neglected wife can leave the partner who denies her rights. A wife should at all times, and by every legitimate means, hold her position in the house, and keep her husband constant, just, and liberal towards her. She must not be imposed upon or interfered with by her husband's family. A woman must preserve an "indomitable independence." She may exert physical force, if she deems it necessary; and women are advised to use their fists, to pull the man's hair, and to kick him should he endeavour to thwart their desires.

A discontented wife should vex her spouse continually, with every form of feminine annoyance until he grows weary, and succumbs utterly to her sway. When her husband passes a loaf, she should throw it at his head.

When all these stratagems fail, the wife still

has her remedy. She may seize all that is valuable in the house, and proceed to a judge, and place her case before him. Let her then pretend that she has been beaten, and show the marks on her flesh. Her evidence must be strong, but it may be concocted.

Kulsu'm Naneh, the Persian feminist, gives full advice to wives on the subject of retaining authority over husbands. No militant emancipator of women could be more precise and more vehement. This writer proposes a ceremony which symbolises the subjugation of husbands to wives. A large brass basin is set on the floor inverted, and a lighted lamp placed beneath. On the basin is a saddle and a pillow. While the bride sits in the saddle astride the bowl, the attendants sing:—

> "The husband is saddled, the journey begun,
> And the beautiful bride her own race has to run."

It will be assumed that Persian husbands are bound to give all and to accept little. But this is not quite the case. A woman must know how to please and humour a man. She should be trained by her mother from childhood in the art of love and endearment. A girl must "store, enrich, and dignify the mind." She is instructed to maintain her beauty, her charm of disposition, and to preserve good sense.

Women are seldom punished in Persia, and there is no part of the prisons reserved for female offenders.

In the preceding chapter I have shown the women of Persia in the light of the experience of Mr. W. S. Landor and Dr. Wills, two modern authorities, and from that of other travellers. It is perhaps a rosy picture. At any rate, Mrs. M. E. Hume Griffith, the writer of "Behind the Veil in Persia and Turkish Arabia," discerns many inequalities and evils in the lives of the *anderun* women. This author hints at tragedies in the harems of the two countries visited by her. She refers to poison being placed by jealous women in a rival's coffee. In her view, "love has no part in the life of a Moslem woman," and she regards the whole system of polygamy as one of "degradation and vice."

Mrs. M. E. Hume Griffith has only condemnation for the harem: "There is no hope for the children of Mohammedan lands until the mothers have learnt a little of the meaning of pure life and conversation. There is no hope for the women while the men are what they are. The whole system is one of degradation and vice."

"The longer I live amongst Moslem women the more my heart yearns with love and pity for them, and the more thankful I am that their lot is not mine."

"Poor, blind, misguided Moslem women of Mosul and other Mohammedan lands! How my heart aches for them! Will no one heed the cry of anguish and despair which goes up from their midst?"

In her volume "Journeys in Persia and Kurdistan," Miss Bird refers with pity to the condition of the Persian woman. She sees only the darker aspects of harem life, and declares that polygamy militates against all the higher interests of women. Miss Bird was allowed to converse with some of the inmates of the *anderuns;* and on one occasion she was introduced to the sixteen wives of an eminent khan.

The chieftain's brides said that there was much quarrelling and jealousy in the harems. The khan sat by the side of the reigning favourite, and almost disregarded his other wives. Some of the women visited by Miss Bird had stars painted on the backs of the hands, on the forehead and the chin. A few were beautiful, but others were ungainly in form. This writer says that at twenty the women look past forty. Many have fine eyes and shining black hair. The women of the wilder districts are healthy in appearance. Their hands are

PERSIAN GIRL OF UPPER CLASS

stained with henna, and they wear amulets. According to Miss Bird, Persian peasants keep as many women as they can afford, and even poor men own more than one wife. Polygyny is said to be common in the rural districts. The average family is large, and there is little infant mortality. In this matter Persia appears to contrast with India, where the infant death-rate is very high.

The women eagerly questioned their English visitor concerning the position of their sex in her own country. They often asked her if she could recommend them effective philtres for securing or retaining the affection of their husbands.

Miss Bird visited the Amir in Isfahan. He talked intelligently on his country, and was very interested in the replies to his questions about the women of England. He was not entirely opposed to the higher education of Persian women.

This observant traveller gives us an instructive picture of life among the Bakhtiari tribe of Persia, who are in many respects primitive in their customs. One of the men remarked that "women have no religion, for women won't live again." This belief is contrary to the teaching of the Koran. Polygamy prevails among these people, and Miss Bird regards the institution as degrading to women.

The harem system in Persia was probably

adopted in ancient times through the example of Egypt. Herbert Spencer, in "Sociology," holds this view, and says that the sovereigns had three or four wives and a number of concubines. The favourite legal wife was the queen. Letourneau, quoting from the sacred Avesta, states that before the Egyptian influence the Persians had a very severe code of sexual morality. The laws regulating the relations of the sexes were, indeed, more strict than those in England at the present day. Resorting to courtesans was punishable, and seduction, sexual excesses, and procuring abortion were penal offences. Polygamy was not permitted. It was not even recognised. Marriage seems to have been rigidly monogamous, except when the first wife was infertile.

Quite probably plural marriage is still comparatively uncommon in Persia through the survival of ancient tradition discountenancing the practice. That the Avesta Code was formed by primitive Puritans is apparent, for it reveals a fear of the lures of the flesh. Polygamy and the concubinate may have followed upon a long period of sexual restriction and asceticism as a natural reaction. The theory is at all events worthy of fuller and careful investigation.

Concubinage still exists in Persia, as in other

parts of Asia, as a relic of the former magnificence of royal palaces. The old monarchs of the country lived in great state, and the seraglio was an essential part of the splendour of courts. No doubt the survival of the harem is to be attributed to this love of ostentation and display rather than to men's strongly-developed amativeness. The harem stands for wealth, social superiority, and property. It is a symbol of the passion for the private ownership of expensive things.

Letourneau fails to trace any sign of maternal supremacy in ancient Persia. Yet, judging by the quotations from old Persian writers, in the preceding chapter of this book, women possessed many privileges pointing to matriarchal ideals. To-day we see that the grandmother and the mother are held in the highest reverence.

Term-marriages, or temporary unions, were allowed in early days, and according to Dubeux, in *La Perse,* they are still permitted. This seems to be a form of the *mut'ah* marriage, to which I have referred. In these contracts the wife is hired for a period, and at the end of the engagement both parties may marry again, or they may renew the intimacy. If the man desires to sever himself before the expiration of the agreed period, he must give to the woman the full amount of the fixed sum. No children born of these unions are considered illegitimate. They have full civic rights, and can legally inherit property.

This ephemeral wedlock is, no doubt, an example of trial-marriage, a fairly common custom in many parts of the world. Such temporary alliances were frequent until recent times in the British Islands, and especially in Wales.[2]

In old days there seems to have been no penalty for adultery in Persia. There have been severe punishments for this offense in modern times. Both of the guilty persons have suffered death. But the cases of proven infidelity are rare in Mohammedan nations. Mohammed was more merciful than Moses in laying down the law of adultery. The suspected woman was allowed to establish her innocence by an oath repeated four times. Moreover, there must be four accredited witnesses to the act of unfaithfulness.

In "Queer Things about Persia," by Eustache de Lory and Douglas Sladen, the authors relate that there have been death penalties for adultery in modern times. At Tabriz, not very long ago, an offending woman was enclosed in a sack and clubbed to death; and there are deep wells in

[2] See "Chapters on Human Love" ("Geoffrey Mortimer") Walter M. Gallichan.

Persia into which adulterous wives used to be thrown. These writers say that crimes and intrigues are not infrequent in the harems.

Their testimony as to the position of women contradicts, on the whole, the views of authors already cited. "Polygamy is less general in Persia than one would believe"; but the practice is not very uncommon in the country districts. Here the men find that more than one helpmate proves useful in tillage and industry. Wife-beating is not unknown amongst the rural population, but it is not a common practice in the upper classes.

The authors of the above-mentioned work state that the temporary unions, which we have noted, were instituted as a check upon prostitution. There are courtesans in the towns, and Mr. W. S. Landor says that the diseases inseparable from sexual irregularity are common.

Schools for girls have been opened lately in the Persian cities. Some of the ladies of influential families are becoming learned, and they are able linguists, speaking several languages.[3] Nevertheless, the status of women, in the opinion of these observers, is unfavourable to their mental progress. Nor are they defenders of the position of women

[3] Eustache de Lory and Douglas Sladen. *Op. cit.*

in marriage. There is no true intimacy between husband and wife. As in India, husbands and wives do not eat together, and in the streets the men walk in front of the woman. I have already alluded to the Hindu origin of the latter custom.

It is doubtful whether it can be accepted as an indication of the inferiority of women. The authors refer to the dominance of mothers in the home-life, and corroborate the statements that I have quoted concerning the respect shown by sons. Mothers are the chief counsellors of their children, even in manhood.

The Shah exercises the privilege of claiming any woman upon whom he casts an approving eye. Monarchs have caused all the women, married and single, in a village, to assemble in the streets in long lines, and they have selected some of the more attractive for the royal *anderun*. The women are never unwilling; on the contrary, no greater honour can be paid to them than to grace the palace. No objection is raised by the husbands, who often receive a solatium or royal favour.[4]

One of the Shahs had a thousand children. Occasionally a European woman elects to enter a

[4] Eustache de Lory and Douglas Sladen. *Op. cit.*

Persian seraglio. The writers whom I have quoted above give an instance of an English girl who became the wife of a Kurdish chief.

CHAPTER XXIII

AFGHAN MARRIAGE

THE greater number of the five million inhabitants of Afghanistan are Mohammedans. Polygamy, sanctioned by religion and law, is practised amongst the affluent classes, and there are harems in Kandahar and Kabul. The bulk of the pastoral population marry only one wife, as in India and Persia. Women are rather less secluded in Afghanistan than in some other Moslem countries, and among the labouring classes the veil is not worn.

Ordinary marriages are by arrangement, as in most Oriental nations; but freedom of choice is allowed to girls who are approached by a suitor. Dr. J. A. Gray, who was the physician in the royal household, says that a young Afghan lover who desires to marry a maiden sends his mother and sisters to visit her.[1] These emissaries perform their delicate errand with courtesy and shrewdness, and bring back an impression of the damsel. The next stage in courtship is a visit of the enamoured youth to the house of his mistress. But he is not

[1] "At the Court of the Amir."

allowed to gaze upon her. She, on the other hand, sees him unobserved from a place of concealment, and closely criticises his appearance, his defects, and attractions. If he pleases her, she accepts him as her husband; but if the inspection is disappointing, she is at full liberty to dismiss him.

The royal harem resembles other institutions of the kind in the East generally. The wives and subordinate spouses are veiled, and secluded in their own apartments, and waited upon by slaves and eunuchs. There are beauties in the harem, and some of them are fair, with light tresses, which they plait and braid. The Afghan type of countenance is Hebrew, and many of both sexes are handsome. But a number of the women are sallow in complexion.

Some travellers have described the Afghans as vindictive, deceitful, and cruel; but such an accusation is too sweeping, and hardly supported by the evidence of other writers. The people are martial in temper, and inclined to act ruthlessly towards their enemies in warfare. They are brave soldiers, and have been distinguished bandits.

Polygamy is not universally approved by the Afghans, and many rich men, who could afford to maintain more than one wife, prefer to live as monogamists. The expense and the worry that the harem involves are also deterrents in Afghanistan as elsewhere under Islam.

Dr. Gray inquired of an Afghan gentleman: "Do you consider that a plurality of wives is to be desired?" "Among people of my race," he replied, "a plurality of wives is lawful; but that which is lawful is not always expedient." "In what way is it inexpedient?" I asked. "Firstly, there is the question of expense. Secondly, a plurality of wives is a source of constant annoyance and anxiety. One wife will live in peace with her husband; but with two or more there is no peace; for ever they are quarrelling."[2]

This philosophic rejoinder echoes, no doubt, the opinion of a very large number of men in the Eastern countries. From the time of Solomon, the harem and the concubinate have often proved hotbeds of jealousy, intrigue, strife, and tragedy, though this is not the invariable rule. Intrigues and domestic trouble are not uncommon in the Afghan harems. A shrewd and reflective man asks himself whether plural marriage is the happiest state, seeing that so many homes are scenes of discord.

Women in Afghanistan possess considerable influence in social matters, and even in politics. A

[2] *Op. cit.*

clever, scheming woman succeeds as well here as in any part of the globe, and the inmates of the harem contrive to rule their lords when it is to their advantage to do so. Frequently the husband seeks the counsels of his wife in grave affairs outside of the home sphere.

Amongst the Afridis, especially, women have distinct power, which they often exercise in an autocratic fashion. A discontented Afridi wife does not take the trouble to sue for a divorce. Her method of separation is extremely simple. She quietly parts from her spouse, and goes to another tribe in quest of a more desirable husband. There is no anxious regard for fealty to the precepts of Mohammed, and no need for legal processes. The injured woman merely runs away and marries again as soon as possible.

In a recent volume, "Afghanistan," by Mr. Angus Hamilton, it is stated that women are seldom seen in the streets. There are frequent intrigues in the seraglios, and jealousy is common among the women of the Amir's household.

CHAPTER XXIV

POLYGYNY IN JAPAN

THE forms of legal and religiously-sanctioned plural marriage, as practised in Mohammedan countries and under Hinduism, are not known in Japan. It is, therefore, incorrect to speak of the Japanese people as polygamous. Co-habitation with more than one woman is not uncommon in Japan, but there is only one lawful wife. The subordinate "wives" are not married to their husbands. They have no real share in domestic duties, and none of the rights of the licit wife; they are in reality concubines, or "kept women," and cannot take the status of the wife.

The conjugal life of the Japanese is not very unlike that of the British people. There, as in our own country, the single, sanctioned union of the sexes is the custom. In England a proportion of married men live in overt marriage, and covertly visit a mistress, or more than one mistress. In Japan there is no secrecy in regard to concubinage. A proportion of well-to-do men may legally and openly maintain a concubine beside the wife.

There is no need for clandestine intrigues and hypocritical subterfuges.

It is not easy for the Western mind to probe to the inner souls of our friends and allies of Japan. We are sundered by a wide differentiation in thought, religion, ideal, and aspiration. We cling tenaciously to life, and most of us dread death. The Japanese are, like other Eastern people, philosophic fatalists. But in many salient characteristics they are not Oriental. They are touched with the spirit of the West; they assimilate alien influences very readily.

Japan is an astounding country. In this empire, side by side with an advanced civilisation, the uncouth Ainus still live as in barbaric days. Culture and colleges flourish amidst curious superstitions and antique customs. Education is free and compulsory, and a number of the secondary schools are state-aided. The training of girls is not neglected. There are State universities, technical schools, and academies of medicine.

In ancient times group-marriage was the custom in Japan. The clans held together, and there was but little marriage outside of the group. Concubinage seems to have been an institution in the early primitive period. Rulers had one wife and many hired or purchased women; and at a later stage the regal harem was established, with an empress as the sole wife, and a number of concubines.

The matriarchal influence is shown in the laws of inheritance. Lubbock and others state that property descends to the first-born child, whether a boy or a girl. A husband takes his wife's name when marrying an heiress; a wife assumes the name of an heir when she weds him. Husbands and wives stand as representatives of property.

Japanese marriage is undergoing changes, such as the granting of free choice to brides. But Mr. Douglas Sladen [1] tells us that women are far from sex-equality in Japan. Implicit obedience is enjoined upon women to fathers and husbands, and widows must obey the eldest son. The Japanese wife, in the view of this author, is simply a drudge for her spouse. Quoting from "The Daigaku Onna," Mr. Sladen writes:—

> "The only qualities that befit a woman are gentle obedience, chastity, mercy, and quietness. . . . A woman should look upon her husband as if he were Heaven itself, and never weary of thinking how she may yield to her husband, and thus escape celestial castigation."

Also, the faults of women are "indocility, discontent, slander, jealousy, and silliness." It might be suggested that these are also the imperfections of men.

The Japanese woman is trained in subordination

[1] "The Japs at Home."

to her male relatives and to her husband. She does not rebel against this submission; on the contrary, she respects the teaching of obedience. There is very little active feminine discontent. The women are happy in their protected, but subservient, state, and their chief aim is to please their menfolk. They are deeply attached to their children, and they are excellent mothers and good housekeepers. They are skilled cooks, and deft with the needle.

Although children are not indulged to the extent enjoyed by the children of the West, they are always treated kindly by the parents. Obedience seems to be a natural trait of the women and children of Japan. It is possible that, under European influence, the Japanese women will rebel against the restrictions of their lives. The spread of female education is almost certain to cause discontent and probably rebellion against the harsher conventions. But at present the signs of revolt are few indeed. The Japanese woman is happier than her sisters of the Western nations.

At an early period in the history of Japan there was a powerful "social purity movement." Drastic laws were enforced to promote chastity, conjugal fidelity, and continence. Like all such schemes, when despotic and ill-judged, the crusade utterly failed.[2] The concubinate probably grew in the reaction that followed this attempted reform of sexual morality. Every man who had the means and the opportunity took to himself another woman besides his legal wife.

In the imperial seraglio the women were secluded and vowed to secrecy. The Emperor was permitted to maintain a large crowd of concubines, but only the wife was deemed a royal personage.

The women of Japan rival their Burmese sisters in physical charm and amiable traits of character. They are vivacious, intelligent and domesticated, with æsthetic taste in dress and the decoration of their houses. In literature they have excelled men. The most imaginative romances and the finest poems are the work of women.

A young Japanese girl is always an attractive picture in her native dress. Some of the women are extremely beautiful. They have small, well-shaped bodies, and in height they are usually about five feet, and often less. The black hair is long and copious, the skin of the features warmly tinted, the mouth small, and the teeth white and regular. The lips are painted red. Womanhood is attained at an early age, and sometimes girls marry at four-

[2] "Japan," Brinkley.

JAPANESE GIRLS IN BAMBOO AVENUE

teen. Boys often become husbands at fifteen. The approved marriageable age in both sexes is about sixteen.

In culture, Japanese women are not in line with the women of Western races; but there is a steady advance in female education, and the system of tuition is improving in the girls' schools. The Japanese women are alert in mind, receptive, and fond of learning. They are highly susceptible to the influence of the West, and year by year they are becoming more Europeanized in the tendency of their thought and customs.

Marriage is easily dissoluble in Japan. According to the old code, a man could dismiss his wife on almost any pretext, such as domestic incapacity, volubility, jealousy, quarrelling with the husband's relations, or for mere suspicion of unfaithfulness. A barbarous ordeal for adulteresses was practised in former days.

The author of "A Diplomatist's Wife in Japan" tells us that, generally speaking, married life is serene and happy. Wives do not resent the practice of concubinage. "Steeped as we are in the laws and prejudices of the West," says this writer, "it is not easy for us to judge of these questions. There is but one wife, properly speaking, and it has rarely, if ever, been heard of that any attempt was made to intrude any other woman into her place." The supremacy of the wife is always observed, and the mistress occupies an inferior station.

Hetairism in Japan is a recognised profession, and the institution lacks many of the repellent characteristics of the West. The geisha is ostensibly a dancing girl. She goes to a dancing school at an early age, and is trained as an artist. When proficient she performs in a tea-house. Part of her duty is to wait upon customers, and to make herself attractive and agreeable to them.

English friends have told me that the geishas are in no sense regarded as pariahs, and that they are often sought as wives. But Mr. Douglas Sladen states that the courtesan is usually shunned by young men who seek partners for life. There is, however, far less ignominy attached to this occupation in Japan than in England or America. This may be partly due to the fact that the geisha is highly intelligent, always sober, thrifty, and more self-respecting than the courtesans of Western lands.

The traffic is licensed in Japan, and it thrives in the towns frequented by foreigners. A considerable number of the girls only follow the calling for a few years. They often save money, and eventually marry and settle down to a staid domestic life.

Letourneau says[3] that:—"In Japan the parents willingly hire out their daughters, either to private individuals or to houses of prostitution for a period of several years, and the girls are in no way dishonoured thereby." This writer states that the Japanese Government regulates the costume of the geishas and the length of their sojourn in the houses. Ten years, from fifteen to twenty-five, is the usual period. "Many of them marry very well afterwards," says Letourneau. The Japanese tea-house girl is no doubt a modern survival of the consecrated woman, for paintings and statues of such devotees are to be seen in some of the temples.[4]

Mr. R. T. Farrer, in "The Nineteenth Century," April, 1904, has an instructive article on this social phenomenon of Japan. He states that the geisha is not necessarily a courtesan. She is well-educated and trained in witty conversation. Usually she is of the lower class. Socially, the geisha occupies the position of the Western actress, and the profession offers many prizes to the successful. Frequently she marries into a high-born family.

[3] *Op. cit.*

[4] Letourneau. *Op. cit.*

Divorce is commoner in Japan than in any other country of the globe, including the United States. The process is simple. If the husband and wife are more than twenty-five, they have merely to appear before a registrar, who cancels the union. Married persons under that age can separate by a legal proceeding, and incompatibility is a valid ground. Marriage is a simple transaction. The ceremony is a civil one performed in the presence of witnesses before a registrar. Young couples must first obtain the consent of their parents. Love in Japan does not always precede marriage, but it usually follows after union. "Love," in the purely romantic Western meaning, is not known among the Japanese. Mrs. Fraser was told by Miss Tsuda, a Japanese head-mistress, and a convert to Christianity, that the word, "'Love' has been hitherto a word unknown among our girls, in the foreign sense."

Miss Tsuda continues: "Duty, submission, kindness—these were the sentiments which a girl was expected to bring to the husband who had been chosen for her—and many happy, harmonious marriages are the result. Now your dear sentimental foreign women say to our girls: 'It is wicked to marry without love; the obedience to parents in such a case is an outrage against nature and Christianity. If you love a man you must sacrifice everything to him.' "[5]

Undoubtedly, male jealousy is strong in Japan, as in China. The almost extinct practice of married women shaving off their eyebrows and discolouring their teeth arose from the jealous instincts of husbands, who feared for the constancy of a too-attractive wife. Foot mutilation in China is also attributable to jealousy and the property-idea in women. Wives must not be gadabouts, and if their feet are cramped and distorted, they are not so well able to wander abroad into temptation.

Celibacy in Japan is so rare as to be almost non-existent. Redundancy in women is provided for by the concubinate. It must be noted that the children of concubines are as legitimate as those of the wife, and no stigma whatever attaches to the mother and the child.

Let us hear the views of cultured contemporary Japanese writes upon the women of their nation. Count Okuma tells us that women were priestesses and warriors in the old days. I have referred to the important status of women in all the communities wherein woman held sacred offices. It is apparent from Japanese histories that women were

[5] Article in "World's Work and Play," Dec. 1906.

formerly regarded as thoroughly equipped for ruling the nation and leading armies.

"Although some of the old-time Japanese women were fond of displaying valour, as is evident from the references in the records to feminine warriors, *shiko-mé,* yet most of them were by nature womanly and of tender heart. All agreed, however, in loving brave men, who deemed it a high honour to win the regard of the nobler daughters of local magnates, and consequently vied with one another in wooing them with poems and songs."[6]

At a later period Kaibara, a great teacher, who lived between 1630 and 1714, taught that ignorance and lack of intellectual exercise was the chief cause of women's defects, and he recommended a full education suited to their powers. He not only enjoined the teaching of household economy, but he directed that women should study mathematics. Up till seven years of age, girls and boys were to be trained together. Girls must be trained in "womanly virtues, womanly address, womanly deportment, and womanly service."

Kaibara does not advocate the usurpation by women of the avocations considered to be in the province of men only. He insists upon "womanliness." But later reformers ventured further on

[6] "Fifty Years of New Japan," Count Okuma.

the path of feminine emancipation. Women have been encouraged to practise medicine, and in time other professions will be open to them. Undoubtedly, Japanese women of the educated class are gaining wider scope year by year.

St. Francis Xavier's mission to Japan wrought certain marked changes in the position of women. More girls' schools were established. The reform in women's education progressed. In 1871 the Emperor counselled the upper classes to educate their daughters by travel.

"We still lack an established system of education for women in this country, and they are generally deficient in the power of judging and understanding things. How children grow up depends on how their mothers bring them up, and this is a matter of supreme importance. It is commendable that those who go abroad from now onward should take with them their wives and daughters or their sisters. These would then see for themselves, and would also learn the way to bring up their children."[7]

The Nippon Women's University was opened a few years ago for the teaching of science, literature, the arts, and domestic management. Count Okuma is of the opinion that the higher education

[7] Count Okuma. *Op. cit.*

of Japanese women is an extremely valuable reform; but he thinks that culture should have for its purpose the training of women as wives and mothers.

He points out the evils of an "undiscriminating Westernization" of Japanese women.

Okakura Kakuzo, another contemporary writer, states that the women of Japan have always secured more freedom than elsewhere in the East. The Mikado traces his descent from the Sun-Goddess. Women have ruled the land as sovereigns. There are more great woman writers than men writers. The influence of Confucian theology was to exclude women from all affairs but those of the home; but industries and trades are now open to women.

"To-day," says this author, "we are convinced that the elevation of women is the elevation of the race. She is the epitome of the past and the reservoir of the future, so that the responsibilities of the new social life which is dawning on the realms of the Sun-Goddess may be safely entrusted to her care. . . . She now possesses all the rights of her Western sister, though she does not care to insist upon them; for almost all of our women still consider the home, and not society, as their proper sphere."

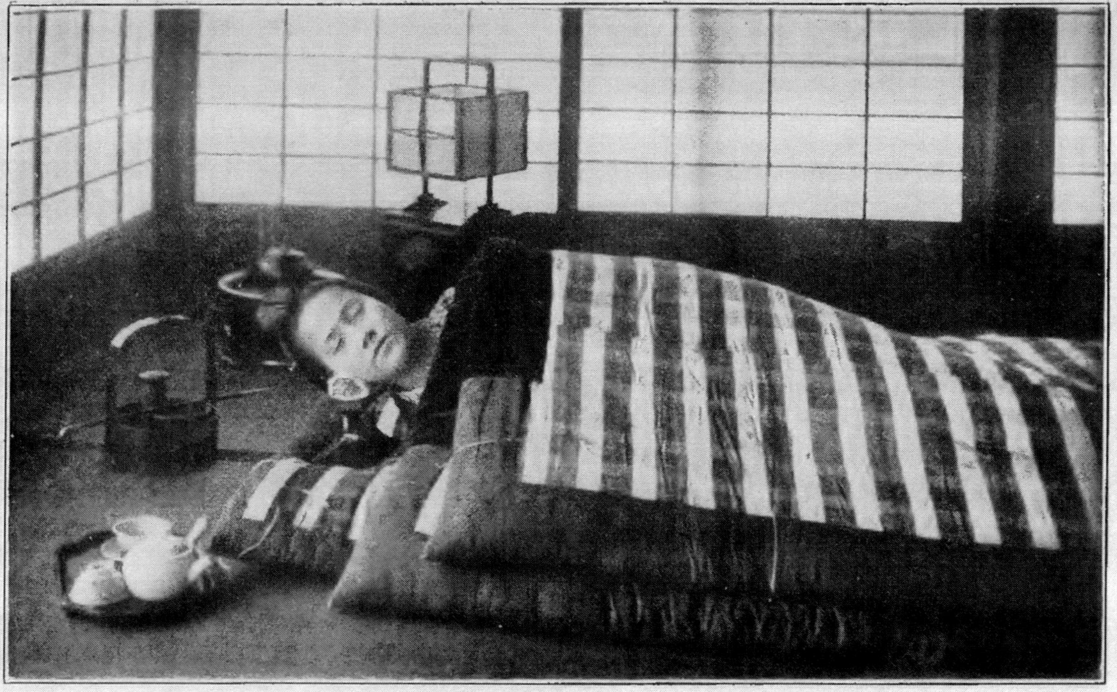

A GEISHA GIRL

Okakura Kakuzo continues: "In the harmony of Eastern society the man consecrates himself to the state, the child to the parent, and the wife to the husband." [8]

In "Japan as I saw it," by A. H. Exner, we are informed that there is less seclusion of the working-class than the higher-class women. The working-man's wife toils hard, but she is the companion of her husband. Japanese liberal papers have said: "We will give our women the position due to them. By a good education and training we will take care that our girls shall be able to fill in the right manner the post as companions of their husbands and as mothers of their children." [9]

Professor Jinzo Naruse, who founded the first college for Japanese women, writes:—

> "The part women played in old Japan was very remarkable, especially *before* the arrival of Buddhism and Confucianism. Men and women were almost equal in their social position. There was then no shadow of the barbarous idea that men were everything and women nothing. Women's power even in politics was great, and history tells us that there were nine women who ascended the throne in olden times. Women in general were not inferior to men physically, mentally, or morally. They were noted for their bravery, and distinguished

[8] "The Awakening of Japan."

[9] Okakura Kakuzo.

themselves on the field of battle. . . . The introduction of Buddhism and Confucianism, however, began to create great changes in the position of women. And yet so powerful were women in society when these two religions came to Japan that their rapid spread in our country was due to the earnest endeavours of the women." [10]

[10] "Japan by the Japanese," Alfred Stead.

CHAPTER XXV

MOROCCO AND TUNIS

EARLY in the Eighth Century the great victorious horde of Saracens, or "Easterns," carried their conquests through almost the whole of North Africa to the Strait dividing the continent from Spain. The fierce Berber hosts were subdued by the less ferocious, but equally brave, invaders. Islam triumphed, and Moorish sultans reigned in splendour.

Spain was wrested from the Visigoths, and the old Roman cities of Andalusia were transformed and made glorious by Morisco art.

The modern descendants of these warriors, sages, philosophers, and marvellous artists and craftsmen are still known as Moors. Strictly speaking, as Sir Richard Burton points out, the modern inhabitants of Morocco, or Marocco, are of three distinct races, the Arabs, the true Moors, and the Berbers.[1] The Moors of to-day are half Arab and half Spanish, preserving the traditions of both nations. There are many thousands of

[1] "Morocco and the Moors."

Jews in Morocco. The army is chiefly composed of negroes.

Polygamy and the concubinate flourish among the well-to-do Moors. The wealthy provide themselves with a number of concubines, who are mostly purchased slaves. Sir Richard Burton was offered a slave-girl of twelve for the sum of £4.

The ancient splendour of this race has departed. According to Mr. John Foster Fraser, in "The Land of Veiled Women," "the rejuvenation of such a race seems an impossibility." The Moors are inert and improgressive; the rich are luxurious and sensual, and pass most of their time in lounging and smoking. Only among the hill-folks and the peasants are men active and industrious.

The harem of the Sultan is filled with women of various nationalities. Mr. Foster Fraser says that from time to time the royal seraglio "needs thinning," so a bunch of ladies are sent off to Tafilet, in the Atlas Mountains, to adorn the harems of descendants of Moorish kings. Usually, the Moor marries one wife, and keeps as many mistresses as he can afford. "They are cheaper than wives, and can more easily be got rid of. The women are in prisons; though, on the whole, not ill-treated, according to Oriental ideas." ("The Land of Veiled Women.")

European girls are preferred for the harems of the rich men of Fez. "Ill-treatment is exceptional," writes Mr. J. Foster Fraser, "for good-looking damsels cost money, and expensive possessions are not to be injured." This writer continues that the Moors prefer a number of concubines to several wives, because they can see slave-girls, but not brides, before buying them.

Apparently, in Morocco, there is no provision made for cast-off concubines. The freed women are turned adrift. In spite of the alleged callous treatment of women, the author quoted states that the Moors are extremely kind and forbearing towards their children. As elsewhere under Moslem tradition, the sons are more petted than the daughters.

Thomas Roscoe, who wandered in Morocco, was impressed by the beauty of some of the harem women whom he chanced to see. Early one morning this adventurous traveller ascended to the roof of the house in which he was lodging, and found that he could cross from roof to roof of the dwellings. While exploring the town in this manner, he saw several houris unveiled and sitting in a courtyard. They were very glad for the opportunity of conversation with him.

During a visit to Hajjî Hassan Entifa, Roscoe

was admitted to his hospitable host's harem, and consulted concerning the maladies of three of the girls. One of the damsels was extremely lovely. The Englishman discovered that over-eating and indolence had given these ladies a rather severe attack of indigestion, and he allayed their husband's fears.

This writer visited the slave-market where negresses were offered for sale. None of the women seemed in the least degree unhappy. They chatted and smiled vivaciously. Roscoe says that their features were not comely, but the women had beautiful forms and small hands and feet.[2] The slave-mart still exists in Morocco.

Disproportionate births in the sexes is, no doubt, a cause of polygamy in Morocco. Westermarck was told by a friend acquainted with the country that three females are born to one male. In the Monbuttu country, according to Emin Pasha, far more females than males are born.

Divorce is obtainable by men on the slightest pretext, and many husbands repudiate their wives again and again. It is considered fashionable to divorce one woman after another, and such repudiations are common among the Moors of the Sahara.[3]

[2] "Spain and Morocco," T. Roscoe.

[3] Westermarck. *Op. cit.*

Polygamy is the exception and not the rule in Northern Africa. It is not common among the Berbers. Mr. Foster Fraser found little polygamy among the Kabyles; but husbands often repudiate their wives when they begin to fade, and marry younger women who are more attractive.

The Moors of the cities are more inclined to polygamic unions than those of the country regions. But many rich Moors refrain from plural marriage, and maintain one wife and several concubines. Discarded wives are often compelled to live as courtesans. Mr. Foster Fraser describes the disorderly houses of Fez as "dens of crime."

The æsthetic standard of beauty in women is plumpness, both in Morocco and Tunis. It is every Moorish and Tunisian woman's ambition to be fat. The stouter a woman is, the more she is desired as a wife; and to attain the necessary embonpoint, girls are fattened from infancy by their mothers. They are almost forcibly fed. In Tunis the women are often extremely ungainly through this induced adiposity.[4] Unlike the roving Arabs, who admire lithe and slightly-built

[4] Mr. Foster Fraser writes: "A Tunisian girl is slim like other girls. As she reaches the marriageable age she takes no exercise. She gorges on *kous-kous,* which is farinaceous and flesh-producing."

women, the Moors and the Tunisians are attracted by unwieldy forms.

Tunis is chiefly Mohammedan, but there is a large Jewish population. The Bey keeps a resplendent harem, and sets the fashion to a number of his wealthier subjects; but polygamy is not within the means of the mass of the people. Frequently a rich man has one chief wife and a number of secondary wives.

I am acquainted with an English lady who married a wealthy Tunisian after he had repudiated his native wife. She found the secluded life irksome, though she was surrounded with every luxury. This lady remained for a few years in the harem.

Mungo Park, one of the pioneer explorers in Africa, noted closely the marriage customs of the Moors. He refers to the stoutness of the women as constituting the ideal of feminine physical perfection.

"Corpulence and beauty appear to be terms almost synonymous. A woman, of even moderate pretensions, must be one who cannot walk without a slave under each arm to support her, and a perfect beauty is a load for a camel."

Park describes the dieting of young Moorish girls by their parents to induce extreme fatness.

MOORISH WOMEN, ALGIERS

Kouskous and camel's milk are literally forced down the girls' throats to produce corpulence, and to render them attractive to men.

The explorer found the Moorish women vain, loquacious, and very irritable. They were often cruel to their slaves. The women were entirely uneducated, and the lack of "mental accomplishments" was not deemed a defect.

CHAPTER XXVI

POLYGAMY AMONG MODERN AFRICANS

I. ZANZIBAR AND EAST AFRICA

THE Island of Zanzibar became a British Protectorate in 1890. It is still ruled by a Sultan, who owns a large harem and lives in great state and magnificence. Mrs. French Sheldon, the well-known traveller, who visited the Island in 1892, gives an excellent description of native customs in her volume "Sultan to Sultan."

From this entertaining narrative we gather that the Sultan regarded polygamous marriage as not wholly a bed of roses. He informed Mrs. French Sheldon that he would give up his costly harem were it not for the risk of losing influence with his Arab constituency. The monarch seemed overweighted with the cares of government and the conduct of his enormous household.

In her account of the harem, to which she was admitted as the Sultan's guest, Mrs. Sheldon tells us that she was introduced to five young princes, all of them loaded with resplendent jewels and decorations. The whole of the sovereign's concubines passed before the visitor in a long procession.

Some of the women bathed her feet as a mark of honour, and each one presented her with a ring. She received in all one-hundred-and-forty-two of these mementoes. Many of the concubines seemed to Mrs. Sheldon "sad-eyed and full of sorrow"; others, presumably the favourites, were "defiant and triumphant." The eunuchs of the royal palace of Zanzibar have their tongues removed to ensure their silence and secrecy. Polygamy here appears to survive in a somewhat primitive form.

The Wa-Taveta tribe of the mainland, visited by Mrs. French Sheldon, practise polygamy chiefly for economic reasons. I have referred in earlier chapters to this common primary origin of a plurality of wives; and in this community we have a modern example of the survival. These people are industrious, and the wives are excellent helpmates to their husbands.

Apparently no jealousy exists among the wives, for we are told that when a new wife comes into the family all the women welcome her warmly. But it is instructive to note that the harem system is not strictly followed by these people. The wives are not all thrown together in one house. Each woman has a right to her own hut and her own plantations. The children also belong to her.

There is no double standard of sex-morality among the Wa-Taveta tribe. Mrs. French Sheldon learned that the women are allowed freedom, and may form liaisons with men of their own status, but not with low-bred persons or the enemies of their husbands. Marriage is arranged by purchase, and there is a ceremonial of the mock-capture of brides.

The children are extremely well cared for, and they develop intelligence at a very early age. They are fond of assisting their parents in the fields and in carrying produce to the markets. East Africa strikes this highly-observant traveller as a paradise for children. We have seen that, in almost every polygamous society, the children are carefully protected and reared, and generally much loved by the parents.

Among the Masai Mrs. Sheldon found a more barbaric form of polygamy. These people are militarist; and, as I have pointed out in several instances, women do not attain to equality with men in a fighting tribe or nation. The Masai set a low value upon women. A wife can be bought for five pigeons' eggs, or a few beads, which is less than the cost of a cow. The women of this warlike community possess very few rights.

Mrs. French Sheldon says that the Chaga

women are magnificent in form, extremely vigorous and agile, and able to walk thirty miles in a day. They are almost entirely naked, save for the adornment of a few bead-bands. Their status is considerably better than that of the Masai.

Mrs. Sheldon boldly interrogated the chieftain mireali as to his conjugal preferences. "I asked Mireali, 'Do you not love one wife better than another?' 'Oh, I like them all, but the new one is the best for to-day; in a week I shall go back to the old, the big wife, because she knows me better than the others,' he quaintly responded." Do not errant husbands all the world over frequently return to "the old wife"? Mireali's reply provides a subject for reflection upon the alleged universal inconstancy of men.

The Mang'anja are one of our subject-races of the Central African Protectorate. They have been closely studied by Miss Alice Werner, who has made valuable contributions to ethnology and primitive folk-lore.[1] Their country is watered by the Shire River, which flows out of Lake Nyasa at the southern end. Miss Werner states that Livingstone in 1859 found the Mang'anja tribe "gentle, friendly, and clever people," reminding

[1] See three articles, "Our Subject Races," *The Reformer*, Vol. I., 1898.

him of the ancient Egyptians. They were pastoral, and grew tobacco, maize, millet and cotton in their fruitful valley.

The men were skilful ironworkers and spinners of cotton. We have here another proof of the social benefits accruing to the women of a community wherein the men work side by side with them in peaceful labours.

These aborigines are of a bronze-colour, varying in shade. They are tall and well shaped. The several sons and daughters of the chief Masea are described by Miss Werner as handsome.

The agriculturists domesticate animals and till the ground. They live in bamboo and grass huts, which are plastered with mud in the cold months. Their hunting weapons are spears and bows and arrows.

"Each wife, if there are more than one, has a hut for herself and her children," writes Miss Werner. "Generally in the less settled parts, as in the West Shire district, the whole collection of huts has a tall reed fence around it as a protection against wild animals. Sometimes two or three of these enclosures are placed close together—as in one case I remember, when you had to find your way through a perfect labyrinth of little winding passages between the fences."

KING WAMBUGOO, EAST AFRICA, AND HIS SIXTEEN WIVES

The position of the women is not a hard one. Women are exceedingly useful in the tribe, not only as mothers, but as workers in the fields and in the homes.

"Polygamy does not here present itself in a particularly revolting aspect," says Miss Werner. "Three to four wives are sometimes attached to one man, but as a rule the number is two." The chiefs own more. It is interesting to know that harem seclusion is not the custom among these people. Each woman "has her own hut and her separate house-keeping." There is very little of the jealousy and quarrelling that prevail in harems.

"Though scantily clad, the Mang'anja are modest and refined. They have 'a sense of what is fitting to say and do, which would surprise those of us who cannot dissociate the idea of modesty from that of a multiplicity of clothes.'"

Miss Werner never saw a quarrel, nor a child ill-used among these people. They certainly treat their children with greater affection and kindness than the slum-dwellers of Christian England.

The Yaos, or Wa-Yaos, living in the mountainous district between Lake Nyasa and the Indian Ocean, were another tribe visited by Miss Alice Werner. They are described as a hardy, tall, and powerful race. The women wear the lip-ring, and they thread beads on their hair till it resembles a coral wig.

The Yaos are martial and independent. They are intelligent and quick to learn from Europeans. Some of them assist in printing a newspaper at Zomba, and some enter the police force.

What is perhaps most important to note is that the Yaos reckon kinship through the mothers, who also dispose of property. A man who marries is expected to live at the bride's village.

II. NORTH AFRICA

Letourneau, in an account of the Kabyles, refers to the position of their women as "miserable."[2] Polygamy is legal among these people, but monogamy is the custom of the mass for economic reasons. Wives are literally slaves. Girls are sold by their male relatives, though they may twice exercise the right of choice. The bride-price goes to the parents, and the girl has no share in it. She becomes the property of her purchaser, who may beat her "with his fist, with a stick, with a stone, or even with a poignard."

In Kabyle, says Letourneau, women are "still in the lowest stage of slavery. They are even in-

[2] "The Evolution of Marriage," p. 145.

ferior to the Arabs, although the latter have preserved, almost unchanged, the polygamic régime of the old Islamite and even pre-Islamite ages."

By way of contrast we must glance for a moment at the monogamous Touaregs of the Sahara desert. These nomads are nominally Moslems; but their women enjoy a remarkably high status. They have liberty of action, own their property, give their names to their children, and marry at their own discretion. The women are better educated than the men. These people have an idea of romantic love. "They strongly remind us," writes Letourneau, "of the times of our southern troubadours, and of the cours d'amour which were the quintessence of chivalry."

III. MOHAMMEDAN NEGROES

The creed of Islam spread from the northern to the western regions of Africa amongst peoples who already practised polygamy. No doubt the sanction for plural marriage appealed to negro converts, and to this day Christian missionaries have had to contend with the Moslem faith. The chiefs of various primitive tribes embraced Mohammedanism with enthusiasm, and the Moslem missionaries won great influence over them.

Almami, king of the Bondou territory, offered

hospitality to the explorer Mungo Park[3]; and allowed him to converse with the women of his seraglio. "They were ten or twelve in number, most of them young and handsome, and wearing on their heads ornaments of gold and beads of amber." Park flattered the swarthy beauties, who informed him that "honey mouth" was not appreciated in their country. They were very anxious that the traveller should bleed them for their petty ailments, as they believed him to be an eminent doctor.

Mungo Park states that the Mohammedan negroes treat their wives considerately, and are better husbands than the Moors. They are almost free from jealousy. The women are permitted to take a share in public diversions. They are not given to intrigue, though their social intercourse with the other sex is frank and cheerful. This writer found very little marital infidelity in the interior of Africa.

Quarrelsome wives were sometimes corrected by their husbands by light chastisement. But the wife in a harem could seek redress if her husband ill-treated her, or neglected her for another wife.

[3] *Op. cit.*

CHAPTER XXVII

CHINESE MARRIAGE AND POLYGYNY

IN primitive times sexual promiscuity seems to have been widely existent in China until one of the Emperors enjoined legal marriage. Children took the names of their mothers. Freedom in the choice of a husband was apparently general, and to-day such power of selection on the part of daughters exists among the aboriginal tribes.[1] In modern days the son is directed in his choice of a wife by the father, who is the despotic head of the family. No son can refuse the wife proposed for him by the parent.

As a result of this custom, "in many cases the betrothed couple scarcely know each other before marriage, the wedding being the first occasion on which the man catches a glimpse of his wife's face."[2] Not only do the fathers exercise this unlimited authority in the matrimonial affairs of sons. After the decease of the father, a son's marriage is arranged by his elder relations. He is never a free agent in the selection of a bride.

[1] Westermarck. *Op. cit.*

[2] Westermarck, Ibid.

Celibacy is very rare, and the majority of the population marry about the age of puberty. The necessity for marriage is taught, and the single life is held to be contrary to nature and almost a sin. Marriages are arranged by purchase; the father of the bridegroom gives a sum of money to the bride's parents. This amount is not described as purchase money, but as a "gift," which is evidence that the selling of daughters in wedlock is becoming repugnant to the upper class Chinamen.

Polygyny is the practice of the wealthy; the majority of the Chinese are monogamous. The labouring men seldom have more than one woman. Only one wife is allowed by law, but apparently there is no restriction to the number of mistresses. The concubine is in every sense the subordinate of the legal wife. If the concubine resides in the house of her owner, her children are considered legitimate, and must be provided for by the father.

Chinese chastity is restricted practically to women. There are stringent regulations for the preservation of sexual purity, such as that forbidding the clothes of men and women to hang from the same peg.

Divorce is readily granted to men who are dissatisfied with their wives, and the grounds are in some cases quite trivial. Nevertheless, divorce is not common. The divorced woman loses caste in the community, and often sinks into degradation. The law does not entirely neglect woman in the matter of divorce; for if a wife finds that it is impossible to live peacefully with her husband, she may obtain a separation with his consent.

The Chinese conception of love differs from the ideal of the Western people, and from that of India. Women are sought and admired for their physical attractions and their domestic qualifications. That is, perhaps, as much as can be said. Male jealousy and the sense of ownership is very strong in China, and women labour under rigorous social restraints. They may show their features, but they must not display their distorted feet. The ideal of the home is patriarchal—the father rules with an uncontested authority.

Oliver Goldsmith, who was a diligent investigator of Oriental manners and customs, seems to have closely studied the Chinese. In "The Citizen of the World" the learned Chinaman discourses frequently upon the position of his countrywomen, and compares it with the status of Englishwomen. He maintains that love is only understood in China.

"Let us only consider with what ease it was formerly extinguished in Rome, and with what difficulty it was lately revived in Europe; it seemed to stop for ages, and at last fought its way among us, through tilts, tournaments, dragons, and all the dreams of chivalry. The rest of the world, *China only excepted,* are, and have ever been, utter strangers to its delights and advantages."

Recognising that a Chinese lover is compelled to accept the bride discovered for him by his father, it is rather difficult to credit the assertion that I have italicised in the foregoing passage. Love, like morality, is determined by climate and racial temperament. The Chinese ideal of conjugality would repel a Western woman, and our standard would have the same effect upon a woman of China.

A young English beau, conversing with Goldsmith's philosophic Chinaman, says that "the Asiatic beauties are the most convenient women alive, for they have no souls; positively there is nothing in nature I should like so much as ladies without souls; soul here is the utter ruin of half the sex."

Such flippant pronouncements often contain some elements of sound truth. English women have tended to exalt unduly the "spiritual" equality of their love, and have too often essayed to refine away the substance. A Chinese woman would not appreciate the ethereal, sentimental attitude towards the passion of the sexes. Yet she would understand the art of retaining her husband's affection and rendering wedded life peaceful.

The Chinese sage corrects the young Englishman. He insists that the Oriental idea of women is much higher than his friend has been led to believe. "With respect to soul," he says, "the Asiatics are much kinder to the fair sex than you imagine: instead of one soul, Fohi, the idol of China, gives every woman three; the Brahmins give them fifteen; and even Mahomet himself nowhere excludes the sex from Paradise. Abulfeda reports that an old woman one day importuning him to know what she ought to do in order to gain Paradise—'My good lady,' answered the Prophet, 'old women never get there.' 'What! never get to Paradise?' returned the matron, in a fury. 'Never,' says he, 'for they always grow young by the way.' Now, sir," continued I, "the men of Asia behave with more deference to the sex than you seem to imagine."

The women of China are taller than their Japanese neighbours. Their skin is sallow and but little pigmented. The cheekbones are high; the nose broad and rather flat. A great point of beauty is the eye. The lips should be thin and the ears large. The outer corners of the eyes must droop, giving the eye-aperture a crooked appearance. From infancy the feet are cramped by the use of tight bandages, and the feet of women are scarcely bigger than those of little children. The deformed foot gives an awkward gait, but this is admired in China. Nature has given Chinese women small feet, but they are not satisfied unless the feet are diminutive.

Unlike most Asiatic people, the Chinese have no taste for dancing. They regard the amusement as absurd, and refuse to recognise dancing as one of the arts. Music is cultivated. The people recognise the moral value of music, and its strong appeal to human emotions was set forth in the writings of Confucius.

The kiss, which plays such an important part in Western love-making, is an elaborate ritual among the Chinese, who, however, regard our kissing habits as "odious, suggesting voracious cannibals."[3] In China the lips are not applied to the face of the beloved person, but the nose instead, and the breath is drawn through the nostrils. Kissing is not practised in Japan.

[3] Havelock Ellis, "Sexual Selection in Man."

A CHINESE BEAUTY

Mercenary traffic between the sexes exists in China, and children are sometimes brought up to the trade. Such occupation is often the lot of young widows, who are not allowed to remarry. On the whole, the courtesans in China have a much lower status than the geishas of Japan. The evil results of the system are palpable here as in other parts of the civilised world. There are houses of evil repute in all the large towns. The women are much addicted to opium smoking. Letourneau says that in Cochin-China no infamy attaches to this life.

The position of the women of China may be described as one of complete subjection to masculine domination. In this typical patriarchal society woman has little or no personal liberty. The daughter is considered a very inferior being to the son. In the most important affair in her whole existence, a Chinese woman is at the behest of her male kindred. Often her marriage is arranged while she is an infant. "The bride," says a Chinese author, "ought only to be a shadow and an echo in the house. The married woman eats neither with her husband nor with her male children; she waits at table in silence, lights the pipes, must be content with the coarsest food, and has not even the right to touch what her son leaves."[4]

There is, however, some clemency regarding the offence of infidelity in China. The law in this matter is not so severe as that of the Koran, though, as we have seen, it is difficult to prove adultery in Moslem countries. A guilty Chinese woman can be dismissed by her husband, or sold by him.

A practice resembling the Hindu Sati survives in China. It is an honourable deed for a widow to commit suicide, especially if she has no family. This act of self-immolation has been performed in public.

China is the land of fathers. The desire for male offspring is intense, and this desire no doubt gave rise to the concubinate. If the wife bore only daughters, or was sterile, the husband felt impelled to take another woman, a "lesser wife," in the hope that she would bear a son.

This preference for male children, which is of the very essence of the paternal family, seems to militate always and everywhere against the condition of women in the community or the race. China is polygamous chiefly because it is patriarchal, and only in a secondary sense is plurality in

[4] Quoted by Letourneau from Huc's "Empire Chinois."

mates attributable to men's love of variety and the force of passion.

There are, however, a few signs that point to a lessening of masculine despotism. Young Chinese men come to England to study for the professions. The influence of the West infects them. I have met Chinese students, with the British "university manner" and intonation in speech, who, except for their features, might be taken for English undergraduates. These young men are the nucleus of a New China group. They are well-cultured and have progressive ideals, and the feminist movement in Europe causes them to reflect on the position of the women of China.

The question of the education of women, for so long almost unknown in China, is now receiving considerable attention. In a book, lately published, entitled "The Face of China," the author, Mr. E. G. Kemp, says that new schools for girls are being built in many districts, and not only in the cities, but in the villages. There is a scarcity of competent teachers, but the importance of educating girls is now very clearly recognised.

Education is compulsory for both sexes in the Chinese Empire. The public schools are under the control of the State. Remarkable progress is reported among the female pupils, who are innately intelligent and apt to learn. In the village schools the girls are taught reading, writing, and arithmetic, singing, physical exercises, and sewing.

CHAPTER XXVIII

WESTERN POLYGYNY

THE religion, laws, and customs of the West forbid plural marriage. Monogamy is the only recognised and permissible state of wedlock in the greater part of Europe, and in all the advanced civilisations of the American continent. Mormon polygamy is practised in spite of the law of the United States. There is no other conventional form of polygamous union in the highly-civilised Western societies.

As we have seen in our survey of Eastern polygamy, there is always a general tendency towards monogamy, and single marriage is the custom of the great majority of Turks, Arabs, Egyptians, Hindus, Burmese, and Persians. Among the Christian Latin, Teutonic and Anglo-Saxon races, where permanent monogamous marriage is the only religious and legally-sanctioned union, there is a bias on the part of a large number of the population towards polygynous practices.

Polygamy is severely interdicted, and in most communities punished; but the sexual association of men with more than one woman, or plurality, has never been wholly suppressed by religion or law.[1]

The restless and inconstant passions of men and women break the conventional fetters, and the phenomena of pseudo-polygamy and pseudo-polyandry are manifest in every civilised state. This fact demonstrates that, deeply-rooted in the breasts of a vast number of Western people, dwells a powerful desire for variety in love. The Church has striven by suasion, and by threats and penances, to suppress this vagrant human impulse.

Nothing could be plainer than the Christian teaching upon the sin of unchastity. Apostles, Fathers, Bishops, and Popes have denounced inconstancy in the state of wedlock. Cruel punishments have been inflicted upon the unchaste and the adulterous, from social ostracism to death itself. But a host of men and women rebel against the mandate of indissoluble religious and licit marriage, and defy the law of the Church and the public opinion of the orthodox.

There is no doubt that the earlier Christian

[1] In Rome Arcadius prohibited plural marriage A.D. 393. Charles V. made it a capital offence. By a statute of James I., 1603, polygamy was rendered a felony. Concubinage was still recognized by law in the Sixteenth Century in Ireland. King Diarmid had two legitimate wives and two concubines.

teachers were much perplexed by the errant desires of their converts and disciples. Polygamy had a strong hold upon the Jewish inhabitants of Palestine and the Eastern alien proselytes. It was impossible to extirpate so ancient a practice in a few years. The polygamy of David and Solomon could always be quoted as sanctioned by Jehovah. Most of the accredited Hebrew lawmakers and pious scribes had permitted plural marriage and concubinage. Rachel did not prevent Jacob's association with the handmaidens Bilhah and Zilpah, an instance of the Eastern solicitude for the begetting of sons.

Esau had three wives. Gideon had "many wives" and "three score and ten sons." In the time of Moses, women taken in warfare became the wives, concubines, or slaves of their captors.

Maimon, the Jewish historian, states that a man might possess as many wives as he could afford to maintain. So general, therefore, was the custom of polygamy that the early Christians were confronted with a very formidable social problem. As a matter of fact, plural marriage, even though it was considered an offence, was not wholly abolished for many centuries after the time of St. Paul. Its occurrence was regular in most parts of Europe. In the Sixth Century, according to the tribunal of Narbonne, a man married to several women was compelled to do penance, but this enactment did not suppress the system of plurality of wives.

Luther, when approached by Philip of Hesse-Cassel, gave a hearing to his plea for permission to marry a second wife while cohabiting with the first. A council was called, and they decided that, as the Gospels do not distinctly command monogamous marriage, and that as more than one wife was allowed in the days of the Patriarchs of Israel, the plea should be granted.

In the Hellenic and Roman civilisations there were instances of plural marriage. Polygamy was, however, very rare among the Greeks, and some writers have ascribed to this fact the comparatively high status of women in ancient Greece. Certainly the Greeks had forsaken plurality in marriage at a period when the custom flourished among the Jews. The Romans also enforced monogamy, and in the early days of Rome divorce was unknown.

Sir Henry Maine is of the opinion that Roman women enjoyed far greater liberty than the women of the Hebrew race, and that the canon law of the Church brought about numerous sexual inequalities.

Until 1060 A.D. there was no authoritative mandate of the Church against polygamy.[2] Even after this prohibition there were instances of polygamic marriage and of concubinage in Christian communities.

The restraints upon the sex passion among the Greeks and Romans had their reaction in the orgies associated with sacred festivals. These carnivals became licentious, and fell into disrepute in the period of decadence in both nations. Out of the orgy arose that other form of reaction known in all advanced nations as prostitution. When we speak in England of "secret" polygamy we misuse a term signifying sanctioned plural conjugality. There is no legal polygamy in Great Britain, but there is, biologically speaking, a constant practice of polygyny. The polygynous man may be described as one who is not content with one mate at a time. He is not constant in his desires.

"The social evil" flourishes chiefly where there is the strictest insistence on permanent monogamic marriage. We, as monogamists, are bound to accept this too-evident fact. Before English religious reformers attempted to dispel the creeds and the customs of India, there was practically no bartering of the sexes in the form which we know

[2] "The Religion of Women," Joseph MacCabe.

only too well. Quite involuntarily, the missionaries have, by the condemnation of Eastern practice in marriage and extra-matrimonial association, fostered an evil that was previously unknown. This is especially the case in Burma.

The European literature treating upon prostitution is very comprehensive, and it is not necessary for me to refer at length to the subject. But it is most important that we should recognise the extreme facility offered for the indulgence of men's tendency to variety by the provision of a huge class of outcast women in monogamous countries.

The institution was condemned by Mahommed. It was banned in ancient Persia, India, and Burma. The Persian "Zendavesta" denounced the practice in the plainest terms. For the origin of modern systematic, commercial "white slavery" we must look to the West. Condemned by religion, by most social reformers, and often inhibited by law, the courtesan still thrives among all the Western races.

The species of polygyny in the West approaching more closely to the permissible polygamic marriage of the East is the intimacy of married men with mistresses or lovers. Such association is of a more constant character than that of the ephemeral traffic with the *demi-mondaine*.

"The double establishment," "the left-handed marriage," the "morganatic marriage" are terms applied to the cohabitation that we incorrectly label as Western "polygamy." There is actually very little hindrance in all parts of Europe and America to the indulgence of men's polygynous propensity. The responsibility is far less here in England than in Mohammedan countries. Although religious ethics clearly forbid such plural intimacies, it is well known that scoiety condones the men who engage in them, while the woman is generally condemned.

It is true that all men—if the testimony of the subjects themselves is to be accepted—are not naturally inclined to plurality in sex partnerships. There is no reason to question the admissions of a large number of men that their instincts are wholly monogamous. These are the natural, the typical, monogamic lovers. I have interrogated very many of my sex on this subject. The bulk have replied that the impulse for variety in sexual relations has assailed them from time to time, and even after marriage of esteem and affection; but the dictates of conscience, the counsels of discretion, the inconveniences of clandestine intrigues, or other considerations have restrained them.

A fairly large proportion of men confess freely

that, from the ethical and the social points of view, lifelong fidelity to one woman is a lofty ideal. But nature, they add, has not shaped them for the restraints of monogamic wedlock. They admit that they can love more than one woman at the same time, and that they give way to their polygynous obsessions.

Statistics in such social phenomena are, of course, quite impossible. Western polygyny is mostly secret. But any man who has observed life in his own country and abroad knows how extremely prevalent is the practice of irregularity, or, as Professor Iwan Bloch terms it, "wild love."[3] William Cobbett noted the tendency of most men to rebel secretly against the limitations of conjugality.[4] The dramas of the Elizabethan age and the novels of the Eighteenth Century teem with allusions to men's wandering fancy in love.

The Puritans strove to suppress all forms of extramarital association of the sexes by the punishment of imprisonment for convicted offenders. Adultery on the part of a wife incurred the capital sentence.

There is little need to insist upon the frequency

[3] "Sexual Life of our Times."

[4] "Advice to Young Men."

of legal marriage with super-added "free love." Every medical man of fairly wide experience knows perfectly well that many persons of both sexes exhibit the polygynous instinct. We may grant that monogamy is the highest and best form of sex-union; but what are we to say of that pseudo-monogamy which is so common in all the Western lands?

In a sermon, preached in New York on the subject of marriage, the Rev. Dr. Parkhurst said: "I do not know how many unfaithful wives and husbands there are in this city, but I calculate there might be a quarter of a million. I would not at any rate of premium issue an insurance policy for more than five years on any couple's conjugal felicity, unless on the contingency of offspring."

A number of pressmen interviewed the preacher, and to them he remarked, "I have not made the statement without careful observation. The subject for months has had my careful scrutiny, and I have found the condition of affairs to be absolutely damnable."

In Russia, Tolstoy said that "out of a hundred men there is hardly one who has not been married before, and out of fifty hardly one who has not made up his mind to deceive his wife."

Other writers have referred to the prevalence of "wild love" in Russia.

Max Nordau, from his observations of German life, asserted that men are "naturally polygamous," and endorsed the well-known dictum of Schopenhauer.

In France the proportion of marriages between bachelors from eighteen to forty years and women of fifty and beyond that age is ten times greater than in England.[5] Such unions are the result of the dower system—that turning of marriage into a "matter of arithmetic," which so often excludes love from the transaction. These marriages of young men, and men in their prime, to elderly women foster the custom of maintaining "amies" or mistresses. The frequency of irregular attachments in France is attributable in a large degree to the commercialisation of marriage. Union in wedlock for love alone is comparatively rare among the French.

It may be asked whether the powerful psychic and physical attraction, which is the source of the highest form of love between the sexes, is usually perceptible in average marriage in the West. Most men and women unite in wedlock for a number of reasons besides passion; and in this fact

[5] Letourneau. *Op. cit.*

lies the cause of numerous cases of post-marital love affairs. The marriage of convenience, the decorous, cool-blooded alliance of two prudent persons, who affect to despise mere sentiment and passion, may prove tolerably successful.

But often there comes an hour when one or the other experiences that profound and all-powerful emotion that is associated with a romantic love. Our divorce court cases give abundant proof that mercenary marriage, and unions entered into without absorbing affection on both sides, frequently end in tragedy.

Romain Rolland says truly: "The majority of men have not vitality enough to give themselves wholly to any passion. They spare themselves and save their force with cowardly prudence."

Ill-assorted marriages from which there is no reputable method of escape are a prolific source of Western polygamy. Most happily-married men are quite content under monogamy, in spite of the variability of male desire. But an enormous number of men, and of women also, live in continual secret revolt against single marriage.

It is dangerous to blind ourselves in this matter. Neither sanctioned polygamy, nor sanctioned monogamy, are adapted to the emotional and passional needs of the whole body of men and women of a race or a nation. There are discontented women, and probably men, in the polygamous societies; but there is probably more dissatisfaction among both sexes living under indissoluble monogamic marriage.

Polygyny is very ancient, and was always widespread in the West, though the moralists, theological and secular, have consistently condemned it for centuries. Among the kings of England, Henry VIII. and Charles II. exhibited strong polygynous instincts. T. H. Jesse, "Memoirs of the Court of England," writes that George I. "had the folly and wickedness to encumber himself with a seraglio." Thackeray, in "The Four Georges," refers frequently to the royal mistresses. Monarchs and nobles throughout the whole of Europe, and in all ages, have imitated Eastern polygamy by the maintenance of court mistresses and paramours. This precedent made plural love a fashionable and popular custom among the affluent. Schopenhauer boldly affirmed that we, all of us, for some time at least, live in polygamy; and historians refer frequently to polygynous practices.

Referring to Western polygyny, and comparing it to Eastern polygamy, Alison writes: "In none of these respects, perhaps, is it (polygamy) so powerful an instrument of corruption as the female profligacy and promiscuous concubinage, which, comparatively cheap in its acquisition, and therefore pervading all ranks, is felt as so consuming an evil in all the great cities of Western Europe."

Tacitus alludes to the polygyny of the ancient Germans. The practice was known fairly widely in Russia, Norway, and Sweden in early times, and it still exists. Long after the conversion of Europe to Christianity the maintenance of concubines was a common custom. Hallam notes concubinage in parts of Europe; and that it was not entirely confined to the laity is proved by Lea in his instructive "History of Sacerdotal Celibacy."

It has been the unwritten law of most Western countries that sovereigns and princes shall be allowed to indulge in polygamy. Anyone only superficially acquainted with the histories of the courts of Europe can point to a number of instances.

When polygamy is interdicted men endeavour to mitigate the restrictions of monogamous marriage by sex intimacy with two or more women, one being the recognised and lawful wife. The irksomeness of monogamy drives a certain number of men to plural sexual associations. Westermarck admits that polygyny is often the result of legal monogamy. A number of writers have declared that prostitution is inseparable from the system of monogamous marriage. Do we not find that in the countries where polygamy is allowed by religion and law monogamy is the general rule, and that the bartering of sex-love by courtesans is uncommon? The courtesan of the polygamous nations finds her chief support from the foreigner of monogamous nations. It is, therefore, not the sanction that promotes invariably the frequency of the practice of polygyny.

Human nature is perverse. Men of the West invented single marriage, but they have in large numbers always rebelled secretly against its inhibitions and limitations. Theological morality declared that men and women must marry for life, or abstain entirely from any kind of sexual union. And the severity of the ordinance of wedlock has defeated its end.

Roman Catholic absolutism in matrimonial matters rendered divorce impossible. Once married, always married, and for good or ill. Protestantism recognised that such a decree was arbitrary, and legal separation and divorce were provided for by the law. Slowly, but inevitably, the links of the chain of wedlock have been loosened, and the new divorce measures show a wider appreciation of human needs. The enforced fettering of the unfortunately married will be one day regarded as a relic of a barbarous age. Until then indissoluble marriage will continue to be one of the sources of polygyny in Europe and America.

Another cause of polygyny, especially in Great Britain, is to be sought in the preponderance of women in the population. The surplus of marriageable women who remain single is often overstated. Nevertheless, there is an immense army of compulsory celibate women. Certain city areas are inhabited chiefly by unmarried women. Such a phenomenon utterly bewilders the intelligent Eastern visitor. He asks, reasonably enough, how we reconcile the boast of our advanced and humane civilisation with the fact that tens of thousands of our women are deprived of the primary rights of love, marriage, and the reproduction of offspring.

This multitude of spinsters might be cited as evidence that polygyny is not common in England. Unfortunately, it proves nothing of the kind. What it proves is that marriage is becoming less popular among both sexes; that the number of men is disproportionate to the number of women, and that men find a substitute for matrimony in polygyny, and more especially in prostitution.

Dr. Johnson, in spite of his stern piety, recognised fully that inconstancy is a common masculine failing. He had no clemency for the unfaithfulness of wives. When Boswell told the Doctor that a friend, in an argument with a lady, had declared that conjugal infidelity was "by no means so bad in the husband as in the wife," Johnson said: "Your friend was in the right, sir," adding, "Wise married women don't trouble themselves about infidelity in their husbands."

Many men and women of genius have displayed an aptitude for polygyny, but probably not in a greater degree than less gifted persons. The amours of the ordinary man are not recorded, as in the case of the man of genius. Moore, in his "Life of Byron," states that all the greatest artists and poets have been "either strangers or rebels to domestic ties." If constant susceptibility to love is a mark of the polygynous impulse, as it would seem to be, then poets from Ovid to Byron and Burns undoubtedly instance that impulse.

Musicians are notably prone to inconstancy in love, as their biographers show.[6] All creative artists are intensely attuned to the sense of beauty,

[6] Beethoven declared that one of his loves, which lasted seven months, was unusual for its duration.

and this hypersensitiveness, coupled with the virility that so often accompanies strong intellectual power, induces amorous preoccupation. Goethe, Heine, and Schiller were born amorists. Rousseau was fickle. It is hardly necessary to add to the list of great men who have manifested the capacity for loving several women in succession, and not infrequently more than one at the same time.

The masculine bias for plural love must not, however, be over-estimated. There are, without question, men of the Western races to whom the bare idea of cohabitation, or casual sexual association, with more than one woman is supremely repugnant. Where monogamy is slowly taking the place of polygamy, we notice that men seek a compensation by forming a succession of single unions. This is the case among the Arabs, Moors, and Malays of to-day. Such a substitute for polygamous marriage is not repellent to a number of Europeans, and as a practice it is commoner than association with more than one woman at the same time. The latter form of irregularity is especially odious to a fair proportion of Western men, who may be classed biologically as monogamic by instinct.

Convention and public opinion, though often lax in the case of man's variability, are still a deterrent influence. Religion also serves as a restraint upon minds swayed by beliefs and theological precepts. Often, no doubt, the innately polygynous man is hindered from indulging his propensity by reasoned ethical and social considerations.

Nevertheless, it is useless to pretend that the practices of unrecognised polygyny and "wild love" are purely Eastern, or confined entirely to primitive races. As George Meredith said, most Englishmen have not yet "rounded Cape Turk." Chastity is apparent, but to what degree is it actual?

Lucy Garnett, in "The Women of Turkey," is explicit in her comparison of our sexual morality and that of the Turks:—

"Monogamy has in Christendom been a conventional fiction rather than a social fact. And Christianity, having denied to women all rights in sexual relations except under the sanction of indissoluble monogamous marriage, the social evil has in no civilisation whatever been so hideous in its degradation and misery as in Christendom."

CHAPTER XXIX

MORMON POLYGAMY

THE Church of Jesus Christ of Latterday Saints, or Mormons, are a remarkable sect, numbering at the present time about 220,000 adherents. Mormonism was the inspiration of a lad of fifteen, Joseph Smith, of Sharon, Vermont, who, at that critical period of adolescence, began to dream and to receive revelations. One day Smith was visited by "the angel Moroni," who told him that a new Bible was hidden near the town of Manchester. Some years after this alleged revelation, the young mystic went in search of the buried scriptures, and again an angel appeared and gave to him a number of their gold plates, enclosed in a stone case.

These plates were said to be inscribed with the tenets of the new gospel, written in a form of the Egyptian language, and decipherable by means of a pair of magic spectacles. Joseph Smith, who was almost illiterate, was assisted by two men, named Cowdery and Harris, in the interpretation of the celebrated "Book of Mormon." The trio of discoverers swore to the reality of the plates; but they were never shown to the converts, and in a short time the documents vanished and were never traced.

The credulity of the disciples of Joseph Smith may appear amazing. But the average human mind is curiously susceptible to the hypnotism of a positive personality, and there is no doubt that Smith possessed a compelling force, a supreme self-confidence, and the diplomacy of a born leader. He was, however, an insignificant light compared with his successor, Brigham Young, who raised Mormonism to the dignity of a vital faith swaying many thousands of minds.

Joseph Smith had several important revelations. He was instructed to start a bank, and he issued a number of bogus notes. This fraud enraged the "Gentiles," and led to an assault upon the prophet. Smith's influence was still further weakened by his licentious practices, which estranged some of his converts. The original "Book of Mormon" had not counselled plural marriage; but Joseph Smith had a new inspiration, and he began to teach polygamy as part of the creed of Mormonism. Setting an example to his followers, Smith lived with several women besides his legal wife.

The open teaching of polygamous marriage was an illegal offence. Joseph Smith was called to justice, but his community defended him against the officers of the law, and a serious conflict was prevented by his surrender to stand for trial. While Smith and a coreligionist were awaiting trial, a mob broke into the gaol and shot the two men. The new leader was the notorious Brigham Young, a mechanic, who was already a prominent figure in the sect. Young was a great organiser, a fluent and persuasive speaker, and extremely tactful and astute. He died worth several hundred thousand pounds. He had seventeen wives and over fifty children. To Amelia, his favourite wife, he left property and a handsome legacy, and all his wives were well provided for on his decease. Under the autocratic and, in some respects, wise rule of Brigham Young, the Latterday Saints grew into one of the finest communities of agriculturists and artisans that the modern world has seen. The early Mormons sent out missionaries into all parts of the globe. In Great Britain they secured many converts. There are now eighty-two Mormon churches in the United Kingdom. Settlers came from Germany, France, and other European countries, and a flourishing settlement was established in Utah. Young elected himself governor of the state, in spite of the Federal Government. A force was sent against the Mormons, led by an official governor appointed by the United

States legislation. But the Mormons stoutly resisted the intervention.

A stronger force was sent to Utah. Fighting and bloodshed lasted for about two years, until the Mormons were constrained to acknowledge the Federal authority. Peace reigned for a time. But the Government were determined to suppress Mormon polygamy. Young was seized and indicted with the teaching and illegal practice of plural marriage. Various enactments were directed from time to time against polygamy, and it was stated that the custom was waning. But this form of marriage survived the attacks of the central government. It is now said to have fallen into disrepute among the Mormons themselves, but it is not entirely unknown in the society.

As the Mormon community affords the only instance of polygamy, sanctioned by religion, among Western civilised peoples, it is useful to inquire into the effects of this sex relationship. Soon after the institution of the creed of Mormonism, the "saints" claimed that they had banished the evils of seduction, infanticide, and prostitution, so common among their "Gentile" neighbours. They also solved the problem of compulsory celibacy of women.

I am informed by a friend who has lately spent some time in Salt Lake City that prostitution is not quite unknown. This may be a result of the decay of polygamy.

A seceder, General J. C. Bennett, wrote a very strong indictment of the charlatanry of Joe Smith. Bennett appears to have joined the sect with the intention of learning their secrets and exposing them.[1] He declared that men and women lived in sexual promiscuity in Utah. Another hostile critic was John D. Lee, who firmly believed that polygamy was an admirable institution, although he left the sect. In "Mormonism Unveiled," Lee states that the prophet Smith preached plural marriage privately after a revelation in 1843. Lee confesses that he had several wives, nineteen in all, who bore him sixty-four children.

Brigham Young was more explicit than Joseph Smith in the teaching of polygamy. In the publication "Times and Seasons," he made this declaration: "And I would say, as no man can be perfect without the woman, so no woman can be perfect without a man to lead her. I tell you the truth as it is in the bosom of eternity; and I say to every man upon the face of the earth, if he wishes to be

[1] "Story of the Mormons," Linn.

saved, he cannot be saved without a woman by his side. This is spiritual wifeism, that is the doctrine of spiritual wives."

Biblical sanction, even in the teaching of Jesus Christ, was discovered by the promulgators of polygamous unions.[2] W. A. Linn says that most of the Mormon leaders had more wives than one, and that the wives had separate apartments allotted to them, as in Oriental countries. Horace Greeley, in his "Overland Journey," states: "The degradation (or, if you please, the restriction) of woman to the single office of child-bearing and its accessories is an inevitable consequence of the system here paramount. I have not observed a sign in the streets, an advertisement in the journals, of this Mormon metropolis, whereby a woman proposes to do anything whatever. No Mormon has ever cited to me his wife's or any woman's opinion on any subject; no Mormon woman has been introduced or spoken to me; and though I have been asked to visit Mormons in their houses, no one has spoken of his wife (or wives) desiring to see me, or his desiring me to make her (or their) acquaintance, or voluntarily indicated the existence of such a being or beings."

Mr. Roger Pocock, the well-known author and

[2] *Op. cit.* Linn.

traveller, who has twice visited Salt Lake City, tells me that the inhabitants seem to prosper greatly, and that the prohibition of the sale of alcoholic drinks may account in a measure for the general social well-being. There is, however, a lack of joyousness in the community. The people are sober, dour, and persistently industrious. Mr. Pocock found a more genial atmosphere among the "Gentile" settlers on the outskirts of Utah, where there is less commercial and industrial activity, but more zest of life. The Mormons are temperamentally akin to the Boers; they resemble them in their manner of life. A sombre form of religiosity pervades the society.

Mormon women, in the view of my informant, are very imperfectly educated. Their level of intelligence is low; they seem like overgrown children, and have no conversational aptitude. This deficiency in education may be due in part to the inferior status that polygamy often imposes upon women. But Mormonism is scarcely an intellectual creed, and its tenets do not appeal to women of strong intellect.

Women have, however, proved ardent converts to the Mormon faith, and enthusiastic upholders of the system of polygamous marriage. They have supported the creed with their money, and given themselves willingly as "spiritual wives." It has been said that Mormon polygamy finds its most zealous advocates among women, and that the practice of plural wedlock has survived through their influence.

The early missionaries, who scoured Europe for proselytes, inspired a large number of women with ardour for the new gospel. Wealthy women left home and kindred to join the settlers in their wilderness, facing privation, and engaging in severe labour, with astonishing eagerness. Young and old women, married and single, threw in their lot with the followers of Joseph Smith and Brigham Young.

Although Western women are usually opposed to polygamy, it is a remarkable fact that many women are attracted to those sects, such as the Mormons, the Princeites, and the Free Lovers, that teach heterodox sexual relationships as a salient part of their doctrine. Repugnance towards plural marriage is, no doubt, deep-rooted in the mass of women in Europe and the United States; but such repugnance is by no means universal.

A lady correspondent, who wrote to me lately on polygamy from the English woman's point of view, stated that there was something to be said for the practice. In her opinion, plural wedlock solved the great problem of the enforced celibacy for a large number of women, and mitigated to a very considerable extent the evils of prostitution, seduction and desertion, and infanticide.

Judged as a pastoral and industrial community, the Mormons are a remarkably flourishing people. They have wrested a vast tract of infertile land, and cultivated it with painstaking and constant industry. Their system of irrigation is one of the best in the world, and an object lesson for agriculturists.

There is but little crime in the community. Intemperance in drink is quite unknown. There is work for everyone, and adequate food and shelter for all. Many of the flagrant inequalities of city life are entirely absent. These benefits have been won in spite of persecution and repeated efforts at legislative suppression.

The Mormon society is a curious survival of patriarchal rule. The system has its manifest disadvantages for women, though some of the ills that accompany monogamous marriage are unknown. There is no doubt, however, that the bulk of women converted to Mormonism heartily approved of polygamy and subordination to men. Had it been otherwise, the State of Utah could not have prospered as it has since the founding of the colony. Mr. Linn says that the Mormon women of to-day are "the most earnest advocates of polygamous marriage."

"Said one competent observer in Salt Lake City to me, 'As the women of the South, during the war, were the rankest rebels, so the women of Mormondom are to-day the most zealous advocates of polygamy.' "[3]

Undoubtedly, cases of jealousy on the part of older wives, neglected for young and new brides, have frequently arisen. On the other hand, the great majority of the female adherents of the Mormon religion assert that they have eliminated all trace of jealousy.

A friend, Mr. E. Rouse, who knows Utah, tells me that during a visit in 1901 he was hospitably entertained by an elder, who spoke frankly and intelligently upon the Mormon faith and practice.

"Polygamy," said the elder, "is not practical amongst us more than in the proportion of one in fifty. It originated with Brigham Young's great desire to keep up and to increase the population of Utah. This was very necessary for resisting the Indian tribes that constantly threatened the community."

[3] A. W. Linn. *Op. cit.*

When asked whether plural wives quarrelled among one another, the preacher replied: "Not often. We have almost subdued jealousy. Our system of a separate house for each wife is an excellent one. We do not coop all our women together in one dwelling. Of course, the separate establishment plan is very expensive. Only the rich are able to indulge in spiritual wives. Such marriages are far too costly for the mass of our men."

Mr. Rouse was impressed by the wealth of Salt Lake City, due chiefly to the immense store of mineral treasure in the surrounding mountains. Many of the houses in the richest thoroughfares of the city were built of rare and beautiful stone. The tabernacle is a vast building, with an oval dome, perfect in its acoustic quality, and the organ is a magnificent instrument. Mineral treasure, rather than agriculture, is the source of the prosperity of Utah.

Benjamin G. Ferris, who visited Utah in 1854, said that polygamy was then practised by about one-fourth of the adult male population, and that the number of wives to each husband ranged from two to fifty.[4] The preachers had "the largest harems." This writer found much illness and

[4] "Utah and the Mormons."

mortality among the young children of Salt Lake City. The children were unclean and seemed to be neglected. This was, however, denied by Sir Richard Burton.

Ferris, who was an extremely hostile critic of Mormonism, stated that the elders of the Church often changed their wives for younger women. Elder Wilford Woodruff frequently practised this system of reconstructing the household.

"In Utah the effect of the plurality system is most severely felt by the first or real wife," writes B. G. Ferris. He declares that polygamy was introduced originally to gratify the sensuality of Joseph Smith. The Mormon upholders of plural marriage declare that this is untrue. They assert that polygamy was taught as a part of Biblical morality, as a remedy for the celibacy of redundant women, and in order that every woman should exercise the right of maternity. The relations of the sexes were strictly regulated in Salt Lake City under the rule of Brigham Young. Unchastity in the unmarried was punishable by a term of ten years in full, or six months at the least. Keepers of immoral houses were subject to a year's imprisonment, and sometimes to a heavy fine also. Publishers of improper literature could be fined four hundred dollars. Three years in gaol was the minimum term for adultery, and twenty years the maximum.

Sir Richard Burton [5] closely investigated Mormon morals during his stay in Utah. He states that the attacks of Mr. Ferris and others upon the community are mainly unmerited and usually false. The "perpetual storm," in which "plurality-families" are said to live, is denied by Burton, who says, "I believe that many a 'happy English home' is far stormier, despite the holy presence of monogamy."

The children of Salt Lake City struck Sir Richard Burton as clean, healthy, well-cared-for and intelligent. Girls marry usually at about the age of sixteen, fifteen years earlier than the average marrying age in England.

Divorce is permitted to women for cruelty, desertion, or neglect on the part of the husband. Men in Utah rarely sue for divorce.

"The Mormons point triumphantly to the austere morals of their community, their superior freedom from maladive influences, and the absence of that uncleanness and licentiousness which distinguish the cities of the civilised world. They

[5] "The City of the Saints."

boast that if it be an evil they have at least chosen the lesser evil, that they practise openly as a virtue what others do secretly as a sin. . . ."[6]

Sir Richard Burton refers to the continence of the Mormon men, and compares it to the asceticism of some African tribes.[7] The tie of romantic sentiment seemed less strong than in marriage in England; but Burton was impressed by the "household comfort, affection, circumspect friendship, and domestic discipline" of the Mormon polygamists.

The Mormon woman's point of view regarding plural unions is especially instructive. Mrs. Belinda M. Pratt, writing to a sister, gives her opinions frankly. She refers to the Old Testament sanctions for polygamy and the concubinate, and to the illustrious patriarchs who followed the practice, and "did build the house of Israel." Quite truthfully, this apologist asserts that "polygamy is authorised and approved by the word of God." She commends the custom as an act of obedience to the divine injunction to increase and multiply and replenish the earth.

[6] Burton. *Op. cit.*

[7] "In point of mere morality," says Burton, "the Mormon community is perhaps purer than any other of equal numbers."

"I have a good and virtuous husband, whom I love," writes Mrs. Pratt. "We have four little children, which are mutually and inexpressibly dear to us. And besides this my husband has seven other living wives, and one who has departed to a better world. He has in all upwards of twenty-five children. All these mothers and children are endeared to me by kindred ties, by mutual affection, by acquaintance and association; and the mothers in particular by mutual and long-continued exercises of toil, patience, long-suffering, and sisterly kindness.

"We all have our imperfections in this life, but I know that these are good and worthy women, and that my husband is a good and worthy man; one who keeps the commandments of Jesus Christ, and presides in his family like an Abraham. He seeks to provide for them in all diligence; he loves them all, and seeks to comfort them and make them happy."

CHAPTER XXX

MONOGAMY AND POLYGYNY

IN this survey I have noted a present-day monogamic trend in the races of the East. The movement may not be widespread, nor readily recognisable in the more stationary nations practising polygamy, but it undoubtedly manifests itself among the newer Eastern spirits.[1] It would be rash to infer from this slight indication of changing opinion that plural marriage will entirely disappear in the future. Perhaps we may assume that, with the spread of discontent among the cultured women of the East, polygamy will lessen very gradually.

The polygynous impulse will scarcely wane and disappear in a few generations, even if we grant that it is likely to vanish altogether in the course of human evolution. None of the cultivated dominant nations of the world have up to the present lived down the instinct of polygyny. Slowly, through the influence of religion, the fear of penal-

[1] Mrs. Ethel Snowden ("The Feminist Movement") states that "the educated and advanced women of Turkey demand prohibition of polygamy, the right to choose a husband, and higher education. The freeing of Turkish women is only a matter of time."

ties, and economic inhibitions, plurality in wives or concubines ceased to be the recognised practice of the prosperous European races. But the cessation of sanctioned polygyny did not annihilate the custom. That which was open became clandestine and furtive.

Diminishing polygamous relationships in the East will not come about through the acceptation of the religious creeds of the West. The bias against polygamy is a phase of the Feminist Movement, which is invading every quarter of the civilised globe. This is not the mere agitation of a disenfranchised sex, but a tremendous, clamant uprising of thoughtful women, aroused, after centuries of repression and inertia, to revolution and to the complete reconstruction of all social opinions, moral codes, and laws affecting their sex. In certain aspects, it is a strife for feminine supremacy. Undoubtedly, feminism is, in the main, a revolt against the sexual domination of man.

In these days of rapid and easy travel, there is a wide mingling of races. The West is beginning to learn some of the wisdom of the East, and the Orient is losing some of its conservatism. Far-reaching changes in the East and the West, through international intercourse, are likely to occur in the near future.

The Europeanized Hindu and Mohammedan, cultured, observant, and well-travelled, begins to reflect whether the zenana and the harem offer after all the best environment for women. A passion for education, for deeper human experiences, and for wider social scope has already fired the bosoms of Turkish, Hindu, and Japanese women. The Oriental Women's Movement will be resisted by patriarchal autocracy, as the parent movement in the West has been combated by men. But it is inevitable that the resistance will be worn down; for there is no plainer sign in human evolution at the present time than the advance of women.

The tendency to ascendancy among the energetic, educated women of the West has led to considerable speculation as to what will happen if women become supreme in social rule. There is no question that an important proportion of advanced women are inclined to criticise the existing form of legal sex relationships. During the past fifty years indissoluble monogamous marriage has been dissected and assailed. I am not inclined to predict a popular campaign in favour of polygamy, under the advocacy of European women. The forceful independent-thinking woman, always mindful of her "rights," and jealous of her position in the home, is not the type of reformer likely to applaud polygamous marriage.

As a purely speculative statement, though one not without a groundwork of evidence, it might be said that a form of recognised polyandry, rather than polygamy, may possibly one day be practised in the West, side by side with monogamous marriage. It is a significant fact that the perdominant sex tends to exhibit the plurality impulse. The militarist patriarch obtains, by purchase or warfare, as many mates as he can afford to keep. A rich man in the East impresses his neighbours and demonstrates his social importance by the maintenance of a costly harem.

We have seen in our investigation that the seraglio is sometimes a symbol of a ruler's might, and that the potentate is forced to maintain such a show of affluence in order to keep up his authority. In like manner, the influential Nair woman maintains her sway by the possession of several husbands. Wherever polyandry prevails, on the testimony of many travellers, women occupy an exalted position in the community.

In the West, dominant, masterful women have often displayed their power over men by what may be described as the polyandrous aptitude. Catherine of Russia is a well-known instance, and there is a fairly long list of highly-gifted women who have shown a capacity for loving several men in succession, and even more than one at the same time.

In the West, the relations of the sexes are in a curiously chaotic state. Monogamous wedlock is only one form of sexual association. A. E. Crawley, in his article on "Chastity," in "The Encyclopædia of Religion and Ethics," says very truly that "at least 50 per cent. of the sexual intercourse that occurs in Western nations is outside the bonds of wedlock."

"The Churches do not help to solve the problem by preaching total abstinence and encouraging scientific ignorance; their attitude is part of the conventional sexual morality of the time. They can aid in the scientific rehabilitation of a natural chastity only by joining hands with science. Western science to-day has begun their work by a thorough study of the sexual impulse, and important pioneering has been effected in the education of the intelligent upon these subjects and in the development of eugenic research."[2]

It is fairly certain that sexual promiscuity never prevailed among primitive people to the extent that it prevails in the most highly-civilised nations

[2] *Op. cit.* A. E. Crawley.

of to-day. Prostitution, as we have seen, is one of the evils rarely apparent among polygamic nations.

Enforced celibacy for a host of normal women, with the normal woman's desire for the love and companionship of man, together with thwarted maternal yearnings, form one of the grave problems of Western civilised countries. It has been said that the higher civilisation simply spells celibacy for a vast number of women.

I recall an afternoon when I sat at the open window of a flat in London, in conversation with a cultured Hindu.

"Probably you think, like most Englishmen, that polygamy is an evil," said my friend. He stretched his hand towards the vista of countless houses.

"In this suburb alone," he remarked, "you have several thousand marriageable single women in excess of men. Is that an evil, or not? In India we cannot understand this anomaly. At the same time, you have a vast, degraded class of women in your White Slave Traffic."

Sir Richard Burton, who spent many years of his life among polygamous peoples, was never denunciatory concerning plural marriage. On the other hand, it would seem that he regarded it as suited to the racial needs of the East. Yet the monogamic trend in Turkey is an indication that the people of that country are beginning to outgrow the polygamic bias. Probably religiously-sanctioned and legally-permissible polygamy may disappear in the course of social evolution in the East.

Such a disappearance of polygamous marriage would probably be followed by a long period of polygyny. History is wont to repeat itself. When Christianity attacked the ancient practice of Hebrew plural marriage, polygyny lingered for centuries.

Lea, in his "History of Sacerdotal Celibacy," says that the chronicles of Christianity in the Middle Ages are "full of the evidences that indiscriminate license of the worst kind prevailed throughout every rank of the hierarchy." Prelates used to levy taxes upon priests for keeping concubines.

While polygamy favours male supremacy, and provides for the wandering amative impulses of men, in its Oriental form the practice militates against woman's influence in many of the wider interests of social life. It is the wastage of a highly valuable social force that a large number of women should be segregated and immured in harems. Under polyandry men are content to be shared as husbands, chiefly because the polyandrous wife has never insisted that her spouses shall be kept behind bolt and bar. Polygamous husbands have rarely, if ever, allowed such freedom to their partners.

The harem implies for women seclusion from the world. It is in a sense like the nunnery. The tendency of modern civilisation is towards a freer social intermingling of the two sexes, and this is one of the healthiest signs of the times. The West has practically declared for full sexual equality. No doubt women will lose some of their traditional privileges in the process of equalisation; but they will gain infinitely in mental and moral development. The State that neglects to use the potentialities of its women, and regards them only as wives and the mothers of children, will assuredly lag behind in the march of nations.

The life of the harem can have no attraction for the cultured woman whose aspirations are for freedom of thought and conduct, and for the full development of her mind and character. To such a woman even the economic dependence of monogamic marriage is distasteful. Polygamy appeals only to those women who are content to forego all active participation in affairs beyond the sphere of the home.

For the ease-loving woman, contented with narrow interests, the seraglio offers an escape from the stress of life. To live as one of four wives, or as one of a hundred concubines, is repugnant to the sentiment of the bulk of women reared in the traditions of Christendom. But this is not saying that polygamy is repellent to the whole mass of Western women. The fervent advocacy of plural marriage by female converts to Mormonism is sufficient evidence that such a form of the sex relationship attracts a fair number of European women. It must be remembered that in sex matters there is a great diversity of feeling and emotion. Women are not all of one temperament. There are many signs that an increasing number of women are dissatisfied with the conventional standards regulating the relations of the sexes.

It is not wholly improbable that the harem will slowly disappear with the advance of education among the women of the East. Discontent is a concomitant of education. The "disenchanted" in the Turkish seraglios are in instance. The seclusion, the dependence, and the narrow environment of harem life are the causes of the disenchantment. An aversion to plural marriage *per se* may possibly increase among Oriental women. But the root of the dissatisfaction is in the repressed and monotonous life behind the walls of the harem rather than in ethical objections to polygamy.

It has been said that though women may exhibit an innate bias for monogamy, they have been the accessories of polygamy whenever it suited their purpose. For example, polygamy has seemed the only rational solution of the problem of an excess of women in certain tribes and at different stages. Such disproportion in the sexes has threatened the community with celibacy and infertility, the two evils universally dreaded and avoided by primitive people. Under such conditions any inhibition of polygamous marriage would be regarded as disastrous to the tribe. Had they the knowledge, the primitive group would declare with Cicero that virtue is but nature carried out to the utmost.

Monogamy, naturally evolved, and not as it is shaped and controlled by religious beliefs, is now acknowledged in our own country as the highest form of love union. "It is not the legal or religious formality which sanctifies marriage," writes Havelock Ellis, "it is the reality of the marriage which sanctifies the form." The cardinal virtue of monogamic marriage is its claim that the betrothed pair are irresistibly drawn to one another by affection. That love and passion are often absent, and that marriage is entered into for a variety of social and material reasons, is perfectly true. But the monogamic ideal is the expression of a genuine sentiment of love between men and women.

Courtship under the monogamous system of marriage is the prelude to union. During this period the man and the woman have each at least the opportunity for ascertaining their lover's salient virtues, foibles, and defects of character, and this probation often prepares the way for pacific matrimony. No such period of wooing is permissible under the Eastern system of purchase, or arranged, marriage. In most instances the contracting persons are strangers to one another; and in some cases they do not even see each other's faces until the nuptial day. The risks of psychic incompatibility, and of physiological maladaption are at all events lessened when a period of wooing is permitted.

In polygamous unions courtship begins with wedlock. Two strangers unite in the closest of human intimacies. To the Western mind this practice cuts at the very roots of the ideal of romantic affection. We are, however, assured by highly intelligent observers that the system of post-marital courtship has fewer risks of disaster than we imagine.

Courtship before mating is the universal rule among the higher animals. It is a natural process of selection, with a very definite aim. Wooing, love-play, and the exercise of choice would seem to be as natural for men as for animals. Polygamy as generally practised in the East appears contrary to the general law of Nature, in so far as it dispenses with preliminary courtship.

What chance of selection has a Georgian girl of fifteen sold into harem marriage? Virtually she is a serf, though her serfdom may not be irksome. In any case, the human right of freedom of choice of a sexual partner is wholly repudiated, and she is merely a purchased woman, or human chattel.

The thousand devices of Nature for the free play of the selective will in the matings of animals seem a convincing argument against any form of human marriage that negatives this free play. The idyllic courtship of birds foreshadows the passionate, romantic wooing of human beings.[3] Even among the polygamous mammals and among birds there is love-making in both sexes as an introduction to physical mating.

[3] See "The Courtship of Animals," W. P. Pyecraft.

The cramping of feminine intelligence is one of the gravest defects of the harem form of polygamic marriage. The harem stands for a sign of that aggressive, anti-social affluence that the most thoughtful minds all the world over regard as anomalous and evil. It is, in a measure, a symbol of vulgar ostentation. Unrestricted polygyny leads to the inequality exampled in Dahomey, where the king possessed thousands of wives, and his chiefs hundreds, while the ill-paid soldier could not maintain even one woman.

It is a menace of the power of wealth that a rich man's money should enable him to fill his harem with a multitude of women, while great masses of the population earn barely sufficient to provide for one wife and her children. It is a low ideal of woman's vocation that urges a Circassian mother to sell her daughter to the lord of a seraglio. The harem system favours such forms of female parasitism.

The ancient civilisation most favourable to the equality of the sexes gave the woman proprietary rights, liberty in the choice of a husband, and opportunity for sharing in the counsels of the nation. Such is the ideal of the spirit of modern feminism. An ever-growing number of women of the Western civilisations condemn the economic dependence of their sex. Olive Schreiner explicitly warns women that parasitism results in female degradation. Mrs. Ethel Snowden urges that, so far as possible, every woman should be self-supporting. This insistence upon the economic freeing of women is based upon an appreciation of the status of the sex in the period of mother-right. In America over five million women earn a livelihood without dependence upon men. Japan has a large population of industrial women. The entrance of women into almost every field of employment has its menace; but the long age is nearing the end during which women had no trade but marriage.

Wider knowledge for women is the rock upon which the system will ultimately wreck itself. This is not stating that polygyny will disappear entirely in civilised nations. Sexual variation has always existed, and there is no reason to believe that one stable, rigid form of erotic relationship will ever obtain. But the spread of the revolutionary influence of culture, a perfectly natural process, will cause a steady reduction of the harems of the East.

Although men scarcely realise the fact, women in civilised communities are the predominant controllers of the sex relations. If women in England elected to live either in polygamy or in polyandry men would be forced sooner or later to accept the condition. The "mate-hunger" of the male renders him, to a large extent, the servitor, and often the dupe of the female. A sex-strike among the greater mass of Western women would overthrow the supposed male supremacy in a few weeks, and lead to a complete reconstruction of ethical and social views regarding love and marriage.

Another inevitable concomitant of the harem system is jealousy. This passion is common enough in monogamous conjugality. But it is even more likely to show itself, in its basest forms, among a number of women equally anxious to win the favour of a common spouse. The seraglio is often the scene of bitter envies, quarrels, plots, and sometimes of crimes arising from this source. No doubt the women of polygamous countries are taught to subjugate the instinct of jealousy. A really jealous woman would find harem life unbearable. But even the defenders of plural marriage do not all assert that jealousy is absent.

The glaring contrast that Western polygyny affords to Eastern polygyny is in the fact that our variety is without obligations. The Oriental concubine, mistress, or secondary wife, has her clearly-defined status and legal rights. Among us the mistress loses caste, and has practically no rights whatever, while her children are punished by a cruel outlawry.

As Havelock Ellis very truly remarks: "By enabling a man to escape so easily from the obligations of his polygamous relationships, we encourage him, if he is unscrupulous, to enter into them; we place a premium on the immorality that we loftily condemn." It is equally true that "in no part of the world is polygyny so prevalent as in Christendom."

Chaotic promiscuity, "wild love," and prostitution flourish under our pseudo-monogamic system. It is easier to live licentiously in the West than in the East, and we should face the fact frankly. Lecky, in "The History of European Morals," boldly asserts that while monogamy of a permanent character is the normal and prevalent form of conjugality, it is idle to pretend that this type of union is adapted to the needs of a whole race. Even such a distinguished Christian cleric as Charles Kingsley declared that: "There will never be a good world for women until the last remnant of the Canon law is civilised off the earth." [4]

[4] See section "Marriage," Havelock Ellis *Op. cit.*, Vol. VI., for reflections upon Western polygyny.

Polygyny, whether sanctioned or unrecognised, has always accompanied monogamy. Dr. Johnson admitted the variety impulse, and condoned it in his own sex, stating that a wise wife would not pry into the amours of her husband. Under recognition by the law the concubine in mediæval Europe was often raised to the dignity of the wife, and she might even be indicted with infidelity. I have referred to the "legitimate concubine" in Thirteenth Century England. Other facts proving an English sanction for the maintenance of second wives or mistresses may be found in Smith and Cheetham's "Dictionary of Christian Antiquities," and in Lea's "History of Sacerdotal Celibacy."

The legal recognition of plural sex unions was gradually relaxed and finally withdrawn, with the result that, as usual, the woman suffered. She was no longer protected by law or social opinion; she became a socially inferior citizen, usually regarded with extreme hostility by her own sex. And so has the mistress remained, possessing only a status among the unconventional members of society.

With the tightening of the bonds of permanent marriage came an increase of the pariah class of women, variously estimated in this country to number from a hundred to two hundred thousand. Is not this of itself sufficient evidence that the polygynous instinct is not readily eradicated?

A Puritan writer, in 1658, stirred by the spectacle of sexual profligacy, asked whether it would not be better to allow polygamy.[5]

There has been serious recommendation of polygamy by more recent English humanists. James Hinton, a surgeon, and the author of the well-known essay "The Mystery of Pain," declared that it would be better to admit and recognise polygamy in England than to pretend that we are strictly monogamous. Hinton, an extremely earnest-minded man of unassailable morality, spoke and wrote boldly upon the subject of sex. He held that a furtive, hypocritical polygyny was far more disastrous than recognised polygamic marriage could ever become.[6] In the United States the Rev. J. H. Noyes preached the doctrine of "omnigamy," which might be explained as coexisting polygamy and polyandry. The teaching was carried into practice by the Free Love community, established at Oneida Creek. Since then the doctrine has spread among a fair number of the countries of the West.

[5] "A Remedy for Uncleanness," by "A Person of Quality."

[6] For a summary of Hinton's ethical beliefs see "Three Modern Seers," by Edith Ellis.

Dr. George Brandes, in his "Impressions of Russia," refers to the sexual freedom of the cultured classes in that country, and says that this principle has passed out of the region of discussion into full recognition. But this freedom is not that form to which we are accustomed in England. It has its serious obligations among a nation where the intelligentia look upon the love of the sexes "as a holy thing."

The born-amorists, the Don Juans of the race, with their marked polygynic tendencies, form an order sundered by physical and psychic differences from the more contained and parental types. Among the historic amorists are a great number of most distinguished and exceptionally gifted men and women. But the paternal man and the maternal woman, the less erotic type common in all the Northern and Western nations, are, probably, the best types for the propagation of the race.

Both classes have their marked limitations as well as their finer endowments. The born-fathers and mothers of the race are instinctively monogamic. Love may besiege their bosoms with irresistible sway in the early days of marriage, but with the begetting and rearing of children come that intense solicitude for the well-being of offspring and profound parental affection which overpower all errant desires. When passion subsides they remain tender companions, serenely content with family love.

These are the solid bulwark of the monogamic society. No polygynous impulses, no vehement passions, assail and distract them. They are the devoted progenitors of the species.

Monogamy grows out of polygyny whenever and wherever the ideal of close personal attachment between the sexes satisfies the emotional and physiological needs of the race. In the West the conception of romantic love is associated with devotion to, and lasting affection for, one member of the opposite sex. This conception of monogamic marriage for the whole life of the united pair arose very early from the instinct of races in the course of evolution, though the strict observance of monogamy has rarely been general in the monogamic nations.

Religious and ethical precepts and stern legislation have played their part in the enforcement of monogamic sex relationships among individuals of the community predisposed to polygyny. But a great number of men and women need no such counsels and deterrents. They have an innate bias to single marriage, and in that state they find their highest ideal of connubial happiness.

No far-seeing student of the sexual history of mankind can predict a total extirpation of the polygynic impulse, even though polygamous marriage may be doomed.[7] The Western marriage customs, like everything else, have undergone numerous changes and modifications through the ages of culture. At the present time the demand for greater facility for practical dissolution of marriage is one of the indications of dissatisfaction with the inevitability of indissoluble wedlock.

Marriage has always taken the form demanded by the mass of the people. Like all things human, the form has never been so perfectly adapted to the passions, predilections, and variational impulses of the race as to banish all discontent.

We live, indeed, only in the infancy of the finer ideals of sex-love. Lofty, poetic, and moral appreciation of the greatest dynamic of life is developing through an awakening consciousness that upon a recognition of the full significance of sex and its manifold phenomena depends, to an almost inconceivable extent, the progress of the race. To a few minds have come beautiful foreshadowings of a nobler estimate of love, potent to overcome the evil and the misery that spring more often from low ideals and ignorance than from depravity of heart.

[7] According to Starcke *op. cit.* polygamy will disappear.

BIBLIOGRAPHY

Across Coveted Lands .... W. Savage Landor.
A Dictionary of Christian Antiquities .... Smith and Cheetham.
Adonis, Attis, Osirs .... J. G. Frazer.
A Marriage in Burma .... Chan Toon.
Among Pagodas and Fair Ladies G. F. Gascoigne.
A Modern Zoroastrian .... S. Laing.
Ancient Law .... H. J. S. Maine.
A Plea for Polygamy .... J. Hinton.
Asiatic Studies .... A. C. Lyell.
At the Court of the Amir...... Dr. Gray.
Behind the Veil in Persia and Turkish Arabia .... M. E. Hume Griffith.
Bible Studies .... J. M. Wheeler.
British Burma and its People C. J. F. S. Forbes
Burma Past and Present ...... A. Fytche.
Burma, Picturesque .... Mrs. E. Hart.
Chapters on Human Love ...... Geoffrey Mortimer (Walter M. Gallichan).
China (2 Vols.) .... J. H. Gray.
China, Changing .... Cecil.
China, the Face of .... E. G. Kemp.
City of the Saints .... Sir Richard Burton.
Code of Hammurabi ....
Code of Manu ....
Collection of Voyages and Travels .... T. Pinkerton.
Das Weib .... H. H. Ploss.

Development of Marriage and Kinship .... C. S. Wake.
Diary of a Turk .... H. Halid.
Disenchanted .... Pierre Loti.
Eastern Sketches .... W. M. Thackeray.
English Rule and Native Opinion in India .... James Routledge.
Evolution of Marriage .... Letourneau.
Fifty Years in Poona City ...... Father Elwin.
Fifty Years of New Japan .... Count Okuma.
Guide for Indian Females ...... Nandatela Ghosa.
Harem Life in Turkey and Egypt .... Emmeline Lott.
Herodotus ....
Hindu Love .... K. R. Chandhuri.
Hindu Manners .... J. Dubois.
History of European Morals ... W. E. H. Lecky.
History of Sacerdotal Celibacy .. H. C. Lea.
Imperial Gazetteer of India ....
Impressions of Russia .... George Brandes.
India .... Mrs. F. A. Steel.
India (The Hindu Woman) ... B. Divatia.
India and Ceylon (Empire Series) ....
India, the Real .... Sir J. D. Rees.
India's Women, Annual Vols., of Zenana Missions
Inner Jerusalem .... A. Goodrich Freer.
In the Land of the Lion and Sun .... C. J. Wills.
Institutes of Vishnu ....
Islam and its Founder .... J. W. H. Stobart.
Japan, Awakening of .... Okakura Kakuyo.
Japan by the Japanese .... Alfred Stead.

Japan, A Diplomatist's Wife In
Japan as I Saw It .... A. H. Exner.
Journeys in Persia and Kurdistan .... I. L. Bird.
Kama-Sutra ....
Koran, The ....
Lectures on the Origin and Growth of Religion .... T. W. Rhys David.
Manners and Customs of the Modern Egyptians .... E. W. Lane.
Morocco and the Moors ...... Sir Richard Burton.
Maxims of Hâla ....
The Laws of Marriage .... John Fulton.
The Light of Asia .... Sir Edwin Arnold.
The Oldest Laws in the World Chilperic Edwards.
The Mystic Rose .... A. E. Crawley.
Memoirs of the Court of England .... J. H. Jesse.
Moslem Women (Vol. "India") Mohammad Barakatullah.
Palaces of the Sultan .... A. Bowman Dodd.
Persian Town, Five Years In ... Malcolm.
Persia: Behind an Eastern Veil C. J. Wills.
Pilgrimage to Al-Medinah and Mecca .... Sir Richard Burton.
Practical Views of the age of Consent (pamphlet).
Primitive Folk .... Elie Reclus.
Primitive Paternity .... E. S. Hartland.
Queer Things about Persia .... E. de Lory and Douglas Sladen.
Romantic Love and Personal Beauty .... H. T. Finck.
Sati: A Vindication of the Hindu Woman .... A. Coomaraswamy.

Sexual Life of our Times ...... Ivan Bloch.
Sociology .... Herbert Spencer.
Spain and Morocco .... T. Roscoe.
Studies in the Psychology of Sex (6 Vols.) .... Havelock Ellis.
Sultan to Sultan .... Mrs. French Sheldon.
The City of Saints (Mormons) Sir R. Burton.
The Citizen of the World .... Oliver Goldsmith.
The Conflict between Science and Religion .... J. W. Draper.
The Courtship of Animals ..... W. G. Pyecraft.
The Crescent and the Cross .... G. Warburton.
The Dictionary of Islam ...... Syed Ameer Ali.
The Descent of Man .... Charles Darwin.
The Feminist Movement ...... Ethel Snowden.
The Five Great Monarchies of the Ancient Eastern World (3 Vols.) .... G. Rawlinson.
The High Caste Hindu Woman Romabai Sarasvati.
The History of Human Marriage .... Prof. Edward Westermarck.
The Japs at Home ....
The Koran .... Douglas Sladen.
The Land of Veiled Women ... Foster Frazer.
Empire Chinois .... Huc.
Encyclopædia of Religion and Ethics .... T. W. Rhys David.
The Position of Women in Indian Life .... H. H. The Maharani of Baroda.
The Religion of Women ...... Joseph McCabe.
The Patriarchal Theory .... J. F. McLennau.

The Personal Laws of the Mohammedans .... Syed Ameer Ali.
The Philosophy of History .... F. Schlegel.
The Primitive Family .... C. N. Starcke.
The Scientific Study of the Hindu Law .... J. H. Nelson.
The Soul of a People (Burma) Fielding Hall.
The Story of the Mormons .... W. A. Linn.
The Truth about Woman .... C. Gasquoine Hartley (Mrs. Walter M. Gallichan).
The Rigveda (Trans.) ....
The Web of Indian Life ...... Margaret E. Noble.
Travels in Persia .... T. Porter.
Turkey and its People .... Sir Edward Pears.
Utah and the Mormons ...... B. G. Ferris.
Wild Races of South East India T. H. Lewin.
Women of Turkey .... Lucy M. J. Garnett.

INDEX

INDEX